Cognitive Behavioral Therapy

— — — — — ❧☙❧☙ — — — — —

CBT for Anxiety, Depression and Anger

Beck Wallace

reader will render any resulting actions solely under their purview. There are no scenarios in which the publisher or the original author of this work can be in any fashion deemed liable for any hardship or damages that may befall them after undertaking information described herein.

Additionally, the information in the following pages is intended only for informational purposes and should thus be thought of as universal. As befitting its nature, it is presented without assurance regarding its prolonged validity or interim quality. Trademarks that are mentioned are done without written consent and can in no way be considered an endorsement from the trademark holder.

Table of Contents

INTRODUCTION 1
CHAPTER 1 - WHAT IS CBT AND COGNITIVE
PSYCHOLOGY?...5

HOW MUCH TIME DOES CBT TAKE?...8
THE IMPORTANCE OF PERCEPTION 11
Why Perception? 14
TRIGGERS AND CAUSES 15

CHAPTER 2 - UNDERSTANDING FEAR.......................17

ADULT FEARS 17
WHEN ARE FEARS PRODUCED? 18
A STANDARD FACTOR TO CONSIDER OF ANXIETY 18
UNDERSTANDING FEARS 19
THE FEARARCHY 20
Extinction 20
Mutilation 21
Loss of Autonomy 21
Separation 21
Ego-Death 22
HOW FEARS CAN IMPACT PERCEPTION 22

CHAPTER 3 - TRAUMA AND HOW IT CAN BE DEALT
WITH..25

THE DEFINITION OF A TRAUMA 25
Effects of a Trauma...27
The Value of Resiliency 27
Can Trauma Truly Be Erased? 28
Reframing the Trauma..29
Reframing 29
How Does the Trauma Help?..30
HOW COGNITIVE BEHAVIORAL THERAPY CONTROLS FEARS 31
Realistic Thinking...31
Create Challenges to Negative Thoughts.................................32
Additional Questions to Ask 36

CHAPTER 4 - UNDERSTANDING ANXIETY................39

WHAT MAKES FEAR AND ANXIETY DIFFERENT? 40
Common Worries of Anxious People 40
Generalized Anxiety Disorder 42

Panic Disorder 42
Worries about Escape...43
Post-Traumatic Stress Disorder 44
DEALING WITH ANXIETY 45
Can a Single Plan Treat Any Kind of Anxiety?.................45
Causes of Anxiety 45
Social Situations 46
Work Anxiety 46
Financial Worries 46
Traumatic Events..47
Control Anxiety by Tolerating Uncertainty.....................47
Signs of Intolerance 48
Resolving Intolerance..48
Avoidance Coping..49
Preparation...50
Cognitive Diffusion to Control anxiety 51
When Does Cognitive Diffusion Work? 51
How to Use Cognitive Diffusion 52
Change the Focus 52
OBSERVE THE ISSUE 53
Recognizing Intrusive Memories 53
Characteristics of Intrusive Memories 54

CHAPTER 5 - STOICISM AND CBT 57

NEGATIVE VISUALIZATION 60

CHAPTER 6 - MINDFULNESS IS VITAL......................65

IDEAS FOR MINDFULNESS...71
How Long Does Mindfulness Take?...............................72
Can Mindfulness Occur Right After a Triggering Situation?
....73
Progressive Muscle Relaxation 73
How is the Body Targeted?...75

CHAPTER 7 - CBT AND DEPRESSION 77

THE DEPRESSION CYCLE 77
Common Effects to Watch For 77
What Causes Depression?..78
The Brain 79
Hormonal Changes 79
Seasonal Affective Disorder...79
Stresses in Life 80
Moments of Grief..80
The Depression Cycle 81
THE BEGINNINGS OF NEGLECT..82

Common Symptoms to Watch For 82
WHAT ARE THE LONG-TERM EFFECTS? 84
MEN AND WOMEN...85
CAN DEPRESSION BE CURED? 86

CHAPTER 8 - ANGER AND HOW CBT CORRECTS THE SITUATION 87

RECOGNIZING THE BODY'S RESPONSE TO ANGER 87
WHAT CAUSES ANGER? 88
ACKNOWLEDGING THE ANGER 89
REVIEW THE ANGER...90
SHORT VS. LONG-TERM EFFECTS 90
CONSIDER THE ALTERNATIVES 92
PRACTICE HAPPINESS OR POSITIVE THINKING 92

CHAPTER 9 - MANAGING GRIEF THROUGH CBT.......95

THE FIVE STAGES OF GRIEF 95
Denial 96
Anger 96
Bargaining 96
Depression..96
Acceptance..96
THE TYPES OF GRIEF 97
Acute Grief...97
Complicated Grief 97
Integrated Grief 97
COMMON SYMPTOMS THAT ACCOMPANY GRIEF 98
USING CBT TO HANDLE GRIEF 98
Be Grounded In the Present..99
Preparing a Goodbye Worksheet 100
Agree to Forgive 101
Agree to Forgive Yourself Too 101
Welcome Changes 102
STRESS FAVORABLE MEMORIES...103
A NECESSARY NOTE..104
ADDRESSING MALADAPTIVE COPING MECHANISMS 104

CHAPTER 10 - CBT CAN HELP YOU STRIVE FOR HAPPINESS 109
CHAPTER 11 - THE ART OF JOURNALING 113

WHAT SORTS OF SUBJECTS CAN BE COVERED IN A JOURNAL? 115
GET BACK TO THE PRESENT 117
PRACTICING POSITIVE THOUGHTS 117

CHAPTER 12 - SHOULD A PSYCHIATRIST BE CONSULTED? 119

OBSESSIONS BECOME TOO PROMINENT 120
CONSULTING A THERAPIST 120
FEELINGS AREN'T GETTING BETTER...121
PEOPLE TALK ABOUT YOUR NEED FOR A PSYCHIATRIST 123

CHAPTER 13 - LIVING A HEALTHY LIFESTYLE 125

SLEEP 125
HEALTHY EATING 125
PHYSICAL ACTIVITY 126
MEDITATION 127
NATURE THERAPY 128
Bird-Watching...*129*
GAINING PERSPECTIVE 130
Nature..*130*
Art and Music...*131*

CHAPTER 14 - PROBLEM SOLVING 133

STEP 1: IDENTIFY THE PROBLEM 134
STEP 2: IDENTIFY REASONABLE PLANS 134
STEP 3: EVALUATE YOUR PLANS 134
STEP 4: DECIDE ON IDEAL AND BACKUP PLANS............................134
STEP 5: PLAN WHAT YOU HAVE TO DO 135
STEP 6: CARRY OUT YOUR PLAN 135
STEP 7: REVIEW AND CHANGE PLAN AS REQUIRED 135
ALWAYS HAVE A GOAL 135
EVERY SITUATION IS UNIQUE..136
DETERMINE THE PROPER DEFINITIONS 136
NEVER BLAME OTHERS...137
NEVER BE OVERLY JUDGMENTAL 137

CONCLUSION 139

Introduction

Cognitive Behavior Therapy is a well-known practice that helps us to better understand how the human mind and personality works. Cognitive Behavioral Therapy enables individuals to deal with stresses, anger, and anxiety. By utilizing numerous standards in this guide, it will help you to stay away from being lonely and sad and begin your life moving forward. CBT can help anyone who suffers from general anxiety to those with OCD. This book will cover all the ways that CBT can help a person lead a happy and constructive life.

It is through feelings that individuals can understand themselves and the world around them. When someone is in touch with their feelings, and understand their motives it can help them make good decisions in their everyday life. Those who practice CBT understand that without feelings, life would not have much importance. The problem is that feelings are tricky things that are sometimes hard to pinpoint. It just takes a couple of minutes for one feeling to change to another.

Everybody has their own particular feelings of worry, anxiety, and stress that impact what they do in their lives. Anxiety can handicap you, making it difficult to connect with other people. Anxiety can be just as devastating. A person may begin agonizing over the things that may or may not ever occur. This is what is called unjustifiable worry. These kinds of worries, if not addressed properly, can turn into a serious habit. It can make people feel powerless in their lives as if they are completely out of control. Without help, it can be hard to feel better. Individuals may wind up discouraged over what is occurring in their lives. Sometimes, that anxiety can make people furious and threatening toward others. They may wind up unfriendly and difficult to work with. The individuals who have been hit with depression frequently don't realize what they can do to help themselves feel better. These feelings are issues that anybody could create. They are issues that will keep them from resting peacefully. The issues can occur for no apparent reason, and are only caused by their mind. Don't worry, there are solutions that exist to help a person deal with their feelings and resolve the issues that may prevent them from living a productive and happy life. One of the solutions is the Cognitive Behavioral Therapy.

Cognitive Behavioral Therapy or CBT is a form of therapy intended to help people efficiently solve their problems. Cognitive psychology is an investigation that centers on how the human mind functions. It focuses on what motivates individuals to act in certain ways. Using Cognitive Behavioral Therapy, individuals can discover approaches to handle their issues. It incorporates an understanding of the issues that a person may be currently facing in their life.

This guide will show you how Cognitive Behavioral Therapy can be used to control fears, anxiety, and anger and other negative feelings that may be seriously affecting your life. With cognitive psychology, individuals can accomplish more and take active control of their lives and choices.

BONUS: Get the free Audible book for US
https://www.audible.com/pd/B07MDDP3XB/?source_code=AUDFPWS0223189MWT-BK-ACX0-138069&ref=acx_bty_BK_ACX0_138069_rh_us

BONUS: Get the free Audible book for UK
https://www.audible.co.uk/pd/B07MGZD6YC/?source_code=AUKFrDlWS0223189OH6-BK-ACX0-138069&ref=acx_bty_BK_ACX0_138069_rh_uk

Chapter 1 - What Is CBT and Cognitive Psychology?

People are frequently stressed, and it is justifiable. Sometimes, people feel that therapy won't work for them, or that it is a waste of time. They fail to understand just how important it is to find the motives behind their actions. CBT is intended to be enlightening and supportive. Psychology involves the understanding of fears. CBT is useful in recognizing what causes fears as well as knowing how the mind reacts to fears. CBT centers on taking a look at how the mind operates and what makes a person carry on in certain ways. This incorporates knowing why a person makes the choices they do and how to help them make better choices for themselves.

CBT emphasizes how the human body works with the human psyche. A fundamental piece of CBT is the client rethinking the issues in their past and pinpointing individual experiences. It is very easy for the human mind to think and obsess on certain issues that may be either real or imaginary. Individuals need to reconsider their thoughts by knowing the difference between what they *feel* and what they *know*. The individuals who keep away from the issues they experience are just going to hurt themselves, as they don't properly manage what they feel. The stress that is created will just turn out to be more terrible and harder for a person to unravel and get over. In order for CBT to work effectively, you have to be motivated. Individuals frequently make the wrong presumptions about the issues in their lives. Those assumptions are often extreme and inaccurate based on the feelings of the person involved.

One reason why an individual may become frightful and discouraged is that they are not confident enough to know that they can control what occurs in their lives. If they recognize that they can control their feelings and reactions, they will surely be happier and better adjusted.

When it comes to CBT, it is essential to find out how to manage and resolve the old thoughts from the past including your childhood. It is important that the previous negative thoughts and emotions be replaced by new, positive, and appropriate thoughts. The individual must know that practicing thinking in a more positive way is really beneficial for them to have a more peaceful life. Experiencing the power of how to properly control your emotions and thoughts is an overwhelming feeling that lets you be at ease with your life, knowing that you can conquer any negative things so long as you can control your reactions on the issues you face is a powerful thing.

CBT is connected to cognitive psychology. Cognitive psychology is a fundamental part of the science that investigates and understands how the human personality works and how it forms data. Its objective is to know how the brain reacts to memories, conviction, and such. A person's memory should be analyzed to know how memories are delivered, what makes them grounded or weaker, and how a person typically deals with their memories.

CBT has been used to understand the human personality for ages. Honestly, the study of how the mind processes the thoughts has been done for a long time now. Cognitive therapy gets its foundations from the past. CBT functions admirably to help a person to deal with your states of mind through specific techniques including talk therapy, real-life tasks, and possibly medication. Medication may help people, but they can be a double-edged sword. Medication can work as a part of a therapy plan, but they can also make people feel dependent which isn't good for the long-term mental health of anyone. Knowing how to control your life through therapy is better as it makes long haul results.

In CBT, individuals who have trouble dealing with the issues in life may battle to remain positive about what they are doing with their lives. This just works with the issues that an individual has. As helpful as CBT can be for dealing with your own psychological issues, it isn't really something that will work for your whole family. This is an entirely unified idea that requires a person to stay with specific qualities and considerations. It is vague about to what extent it would take for CBT to work. It may take a long time for CBT to benefit a person. It is through CBT that it ends up less demanding for a person to have a controlled and practical life. The individuals who take an interest in CBT sessions will talk more about what they can do to develop and to be better, more grounded, and more joyful individuals. What's more important is that this keeps issues like dread, nervousness, and different issues from becoming a great concern. A person who is experiencing depression might encounter self-destructive thoughts or activities. They are the ones that would need to get propelled types of therapy and support including medicines and hospitalization.

How Much Time Does CBT Take?

Everybody reacts to cognitive therapy in their own way. A few people may improve the situation with mental therapy by working with their specialists. CBT can take weeks or even months to finish. It is up to the individual to choose what one needs to finish CBT and how long the work may take. The individuals who are patient and willing to work at it will profit the most from what CBT can bring. It is through your work and plans for CBT that it ends up easier for somebody to develop and flourish as a person. Obviously, there are issues that accompany CBT. However, the positives encompassing the training are significantly more noteworthy than any negative issues. It is more encouraging for individuals to see how well CBT can help in any circumstance.

The individuals who wish to use CBT should consider what they are doing on a daily basis. This is a training that is extremely convoluted and involves heaps of exertion on a patient's end. In any case, the individuals who are fit for flourishing and developing will develop into being better individuals. The means in CBT can be broad and, at times, a little confusing. It is through CBT that a person can advance and be a more grounded person.

The evaluation process of CBT is expected to recognize an upsetting circumstance toward the beginning. Each individual has his or her own circumstance that may cause mental issues. The circumstance can be anything that somebody may battle with. For example, a person may be focused on things like fearing something specific. That individual could likewise express indignation toward others or certain circumstances. CBT makes a solid collision between the member and any individual who may help. Regardless of whether it is working with an advisor or essentially talking it over with other individuals or even with oneself, it ends up easier for CBT to be utilized.

The evaluation procedure can take as much time as needed. The objective is to fully understand the person's mind. Then, you can discover how to make positive changes. A helpful plan should be developed during the evaluation procedure. It is the place the individual who experiences CBT will feel certain about the procedure so that they will confide in any their therapist. It is the only way for CBT to help. This feeling of trust is crucial as it identifies with how positive your state of mind may be. The key is that a person will feel good chatting with somebody that is confident and knowledgeable in CBT. Knowing how well the procedure will function and getting a straightforward understanding is fundamental to having a superior involvement in dealing with your intense emotions and concerns. There might be times when an expert directs CBT and other times where the individual might choose to go through CBT techniques on their own. There are benefits and drawbacks for both options. Using a CBT therapist is particularly useful for situations when a person has huge issues and maybe has a danger of self-harm or potentially hurt other individuals and thus requires extra help with dealing with their mental issues.

The following stage is the perceiving and assessing stage. This is all about the thoughts one has. The evaluation ought to have figured out what the issues are. It is currently time to go inside and out to perceive what has made those issues develop. The objective is to decide how the upsetting circumstance began. CBT centers on the idea in cognitive psychology where a person may begin to feel distressed or stressed over things in life due to past occasions. In some cases, it could happen because of physical abuse, a separation, a death in the family, bullying, or whatever else that may be troublesome for somebody to deal with. Whatever the case might be, the base of the issue must be investigated to understand what somebody is considering and how those contemplations are carried out. This procedure is regularly difficult. It is difficult to figure out your where thoughts starts and where it ends. By knowing how those thoughts are processing and what is making them advance and change, makes it easier for a person to have more authority over your life. At the point when a person experiences CBT long enough, they begin to see patterns and themes in their thoughts. These may identify with what one may think or how positive somebody may be over some activities or occasions throughout everyday life. The procedures may involve recording every one of the feelings or changes that somebody is experiencing at a specific time. There must be a feeling of transparency all throughout the evaluation procedure. A person who is in therapy must have their needs evaluated to help with perceiving the necessities that somebody has and in choosing is possible to determine certain psychological issues.

The Importance of Perception

Individuals will come into contact with different improvements in their daily lives. They will see one-of-a-kind things, smell different fragrances, taste different foods, and hear sounds in their homes and outside. It is through a person's recognition that things can be distinguished. The essential meaning of observation is that it is the demonstration of seeing what is in nature. While recognition is frequently connected with the physical things that somebody may understand, this idea is more than that. Observation is additionally about how individuals translate certain ideas. Here's a short case of how somebody may see things. A car is moving along the road. One individual may state, "Take a look at that car not far from us." The second individual may be more particular and see something additional about the vehicle. That somebody would state, "Take a look at that blue car moving along the street." A third individual may be much more discerning, taking a look at a portion of the particular highlights that can be found on that car. The individual may see that the vehicle isn't just a car but an extravagant BMW sports car. The third individual would state, "Take a look at that new blue BMW not too far from us." The third individual is the most discerning individual in this situation.

While the first two individuals are seeing the fundamental things about the car, the third person noticed the particular sort of car and that it is made by a specific car brand. That third individual may have seen something intriguing encompassing that car. Anyway, what does discernment have to do with CBT? It is through the observation that a person can distinguish what somebody may feel. It is the detail of what is making somebody be anxious or stressed over something. The craft of recognition is vital to perceive. With CBT, individuals need to see the issues that have made them act in certain ways. They have to see what they are doing and why their lives have changed due to specific issues in their lives. The key piece of recognition for cognitive therapy includes the procedures used to figure out what a person may do or encounter. Everybody has the ability to watch things from numerous points of view in light of their faculties of sight, taste, hearing, et cetera. Everybody has their own advantages that figure out what they see. A few people may see birds and can recognize every species if that is the thing that they are keen on. Someone else may just have the capacity to see that they hear a warbler yet have not the possibility of the types of birds, nor do they care since it isn't what intrigues them. There is a rule when a person may be propelled to take after specific thoughts in light of the things one sees and how somebody translates it.

One way of identifying with the cognitive idea is structuralism. This is a field that spotlights on how individuals see certain thoughts or qualities. Structuralism is a training that focuses on what individuals may think about while in a general condition of awareness. The most straightforward ideas might be utilized to distinguish what somebody is thinking or feeling.

In spite of the fact that it isn't utilized as regularly as different hypotheses, structuralism may at present be utilized to see how individuals translate things and occasions. The objective of structuralism is to survey a person's cognizance and how it is changing and developing. For example, a person may be given a specific thing or boost. They are requested to depict what it resembles. The words and emotions that are evoked by the upgrade can be utilized to comprehend what that individual may think or feel. The vibes that a person feels while seeing something may likewise be investigated in the training. These sensations frequently happen when somebody takes a look at a particular item and comments on something that he notices about the item. A person could be given a specific item and is asked to questions that will evaluate how they feel about the item being shown. Knowing how to express your qualities or thoughts regarding what they see can demonstrate hidden qualities and inclinations. Structuralism isn't exactly mainstream today, however, could still be utilized to see how a person may feel around one tangible thing versus another. It could help decide the thoughts that a person can use to fight off negative emotions.

Why Perception?

Despite the fact that there are a variety of ways that can be used in Cognitive Behavioral Therapy, it is vital to use those methods to get pieces of information about what somebody may feel. At first glance, a person's feelings of trepidation or different stresses might be affirmed through recognition. Those feelings of trepidation and concerns may likewise be affirmed in view of how a person may react to specific issues. Knowing how recognition functions are basic to comprehend what somebody fears and regards versus what somebody may be all right with. The use of recognition gives individuals an idea of what's in store when managing others. The focus of Cognitive Behavioral Therapy centers around what individuals can do to develop and flourish by understanding what they are doing and why.

Triggers and Causes

A person might experience a trigger after going  through one of the many causes developing anxiety or a fear. Knowing the trigger is vital to discovering the cause that might take place and make a situation worse. The human brain is complicated and several triggers might occur at a time. The main goal of handling triggers is to look at which ones might be the strongest. Keep a list of occasions when a fear is triggered to identify what the main triggers might be.

Chapter 2 - Understanding Fear

Some individuals also like to claim that they don't have any fears, yet deep down; there are most likely several things that activate fears or concerns in a person's mind.

Sometimes, imaginary fears may develop. The classic fear of monsters under the bed is common at this point.

Adult Fears

Just because most fears develop in children does not mean they also cannot develop in adults. It is true that adults are not as likely to experience new fears, but at the same time, they might be likely to experience fears due to changing circumstances: an elderly person might see many friends and family members in your life dying.

For cognitive psychology to work when treating a person's fears, it is vital to be aware of what someone is afraid of. It is natural for people to hide and try what they fear because they are either uncomfortable with it or they are too afraid to admit that they have certain fears.

When Are Fears Produced?

It is easier for people to develop fears and other strong long-term feelings when they are at a young age. Fears can develop at an early age and can become more concrete as a person ages and becomes more aware of some of the things that might cause a fear to develop. Fears are often likely to develop at certain times. They may occur from direct contact with something. This includes a contact that left a negative impact on one's mind. They might develop when something bad happens to someone who is very close to another person. Some fears happen from reading or hearing stories about something frightening. They might happen by association. When a person's spouse or sibling feels a fear, that other person might start to feel the same fear. All people respond to these fears in different ways. The struggles that can occur could be dramatic. The development of fears is important to understand when it comes to resolving them through cognitive psychology. It is also important to recall some of the memories that one has about something that might not be as pervasive but could still make an impact.

A Standard Factor to Consider of Anxiety

Worry is an all-natural component of life. Some individuals also like to assert that they are absolutely afraid of nothing. However, deep within them, there are still some lingering fears that are maybe unbeknownst to them or they may be aware of but are afraid to admit it. Too much concern of an individual brings them constant worry.

Every individual creates brand new concerns at numerous phases in their lives. These concerns could be created at numerous times in somebody's life. However, the certain nature of the worry, as well as the frequency of thinking about it, could be varied based on age as well as just how reasonable they are regarding their anxieties. The mind can be too preoccupied with the fear when someone is trying to figure out the situation at hand and how to resolve the worries or other issues.

Understanding Fears

A simple search online will reveal that there are hundreds of fears that people may exhibit in their lives. There are plenty of common fears like arachnophobia (fear of spiders), acrophobia (fear of heights), cynophobia (fear of dogs), and aviophobia (fear of flying). There are also some unusual fears that people hold. A person might have a fear of making decisions. Someone might also have gephyrophobia, a fear of bridges. Some fears are especially strange. Some people may suffer from nomophobia, a fear of going somewhere without a mobile phone or unable to use one. Others may experience somniphobia, a fear of falling asleep. In short, with all the different things in the world, there is absolutely a fear that could be attached to any of it. The extent of one's fear might vary depending on someone's experiences. It is through conditioning that a person will have an easier time with managing one's life and one's fears.

The Feararchy

There are five fears that are shared among people throughout society. Each of these fears builds upon one another into what is known as a Feararchy. Composed by Dr. Karl Albrecht, the Feararchy is a hierarchy that focuses on five fears that people may experience. These features are listed from first to fifth with the first being the base of the pyramid that the Feararchy is on and the fifth being the peak where all fears eventually end up.

Extinction

The most basic fear of the Feararchy pyramid is the fear of extinction. This is another way of saying that a person is afraid of death. Everyone worries about death at some point. Some people might be afraid of situations that they feel could put their lives in jeopardy. These include people who are afraid of boarding buses or airplanes or people who don't want to be in tall buildings. When a person thinks about the potential of death, they start to be afraid and worried about what might happen and the impact of one's death on other people. The fear of extinction may be threatening to people with families. A person might worry about what might happen to one's siblings, parents, spouse, or other people who are close to that person's life.

Mutilation

A fear of mutilation is often as intense as the fear of extinction. People are frequently afraid of what would happen if their bodies were permanently impacted by something outside of their control. The fear of mutilation is the fear of having one's body injured. This includes fears of one's body parts, organs, and other features being hurt. Sometimes, people might become afraid of various animals out of the fear that those animals are going to mutilate them.

Loss of Autonomy

The loss of autonomy refers to the fear of being paralyzed or trapped in some way. People want to have full control over their bodies, but it becomes easy for people to lose that control from illness or from violent acts. A loss of autonomy does not have to be strictly physical in nature. This loss may also happen when a person has no control over their relationships or social situations. That person might not be given many choices as to where to go or with whom to talk.

Separation

The best way to explain separation is that it is where a person is not wanted or respected by other people. In many cases, this might be a person getting the silent treatment from others. A person is rejected, abandoned, or otherwise ignored by other people. This is a highly psychological fear that focuses on how dependent a person is on someone else. When that dependence is lost or fractured, it becomes harder for a person to feel comfortable with what can happen in life. For instance, a person who has been married to someone for fifty years might be afraid of losing the person they married. The separation that occurs would make it harder for a person to feel happy about one's situation and circumstances in life.

Ego-Death

This is a person's fear of being ashamed, humiliated or any other forms of self-disapproval that can threaten the loss of the person's self-integrity. It is the fear of disintegration and shattering of an individual's sense of worthiness, capabilities, and lovability.

How Fears Can Impact Perception

It is through fear that a person's perception will quickly be impacted. When someone fears something, their perception becomes increasingly negative to the point where they try to avoid certain situations. A person who sees something that they are afraid of will develop added stress in the amygdala. As this area of the brain functions, it produces a sense of fear or worry in one's mind. This makes it difficult for people to feel comfortable about the situation they face that is causing fear. The pressure within the amygdala comes from the sensory organs of the body noticing the sight, scents, sounds, and other physical characteristics of whatever someone is afraid of. The amygdala may be connected to the part of the brain that manages one's senses, although further research is needed to fully understand this concept. As the fearful stimuli are introduced, it becomes easier for a person to become afraid and worried. The stimuli will cause a person to become afraid and concerned. The worry that is produced can be damaging as it keeps that person from being capable of seeing something for what it is in reality.

Chapter 3 - Trauma and How It Can Be Dealt With

There are, oftentimes, when a person might suffer from a trauma that causes them to become afraid. A trauma is something that triggers fears, causes people to become depressed, or even prompts a person to feel extensive grief for a long time. Understanding what trauma is and how it can directly influence one's life should be explored to understand what causes a person to have certain problems in life.

The Definition of a Trauma

Trauma is an event that might come out of nowhere and create a significant worry in one's life. This is a threat that took place in the past and has caused a person to become unhealthy or unhappy. It will make life difficult as a person struggles to figure out how one's behaviors may be changed because of the trauma. Knowing how the trauma is produced helps to understand how this part of the human thinking pattern works. Traumas can happen in many ways and will more than likely happen without warning. It is through the sudden pains and worries produced by the trauma that it becomes harder for someone to carry on a normal life. There are many types of trauma that someone could experience: Car accidents, sporting-related accidents, and many other accidents that cause injury can create trauma. The pains that came from being hurt could be too much for some people to bear. Medical-related problems do not have to be direct injuries. Traumas can occur when a person suffers from rare diseases or other issues that required extensive treatments, surgery, or hospitalization.

Relational trauma is a situation where someone has problems with one's romantic or personal life. Common forms of relational trauma are abuse or neglect by a spouse. Natural disasters can cause traumas such as an earthquake, hurricane, tornado, or something else that places one's sanity and safety in immediate jeopardy. Conditions relating to war can cause trauma, particularly those who are in the military or people from countries where war has been a persistent issue. People might see difficult or painful things in war or may be subject to harmful living conditions. Poverty is an issue that keeps people from being healthy or capable of managing their lives in a reasonable fashion. The trauma from poverty can increase when that person suffers poverty for a long period of time. Adverse childhood events can make an impact. As the brain evolves, it becomes easier for a child to not fully understand what is happening during certain events. This could cause a child to feel emotionally distressed. All of these problems can happen at any age, but they are issues that can create a great deal of emotional scarring. The impacts can be devastating and might be difficult for some people to recover. For instance, it might be a challenge for a person to get beyond a trauma due to the long-term effects or the ongoing dread that something like this could happen again. The fact that traumas can cause fears in many people based on what happened can directly influence what people might feel.

Effects of a Trauma

Trauma has many effects, although the specific problems produced will vary by each person. A person's safety may be threatened due to some trauma that occurred. That person could feel that the trauma might happen again. That someone's sanity may also be compromised. They might be afraid of what might happen and be emotionally scarred. The human body may also be impacted. Sometimes, a trauma might cause long-term damage to the body or instill the fear that the damage could be permanent. The problems that persist with trauma can be devastating and in some cases, will last for one's lifetime. It is through the trauma that one experiences that it can become difficult for anyone to live a positive and controlled life.

The Value of Resiliency

Although trauma can be difficult to deal with, that does not mean that a person cannot recover from the trauma experienced. Resiliency refers to how well a person is capable of getting beyond the trauma to live comfortably. The human mind is resilient enough and a person will have a chance of recovering and move forward with one's life. Let's look at the things that can happen through resiliency.

Natural supports in one's life can be utilized to improve what one might be thinking and doing in their life. People can do things in their lives to help themselves. These include things that help people to be more proficient and productive while feeling positive about what they want to do for themselves. People can manage their feelings and keep them under control including looking into how those feelings are modulated and kept in check. There are always positive connections that can be made in one's life. These include connections that focus on how well one's life can be managed and kept positive. The most important thing is that a person will realize that he or she is worthy of life. This includes understanding that there are always things in the world for people to look forward to. It is vital for people to look at what they are doing to be resilient and ready to respond to anything that happens.

Can Trauma Truly Be Erased?

As easy as it may be for the brain to manage trauma and recover, there are times when it might be impossible for trauma to be erased completely. The greater concern is that the trauma that is produced might be deep and well-rooted in the mind. The threat involved can be dramatic depending on how intense the situation was and how long ago the trauma took place. The memories that surround the trauma are often difficult to repair. The worst part is that the effects of the trauma might remain throughout one's life. For instance, a car wreck might have resulted in a permanent injury. A broken relationship might have led to someone feeling insecure. A major natural disaster might have caused the destruction of one's home. In other words, there is a chance that the trauma that is produced could be a challenge to manage, but it is through that worry that someone might be at risk of harm. The best thing that can be done for managing trauma is to work harder to find the root of the trauma and to address the fear that was a result. This is all about ensuring that the trauma of a situation can be kept under control and not be a threat to one's life.

Reframing the Trauma

There is always going to be some problem in one's life that will cause anxiety or fear to develop. A traumatic experience can cause anyone to feel fear, anger, grief, and depression and can lead to a condition such as PTSD. There comes a need to look at how the trauma evolved and what can be done to correct or soften the effects of the issue.

Reframing

 Reframing is a process when someone looks at a certain situation from a new point of view. As the human mind changes, events, and situations will be seen differently. Reframing is a way for someone to manage their emotions and thoughts.

There are many ways a person can work toward reframing thoughts. Knowing how these issues can be managed will help people understand their thinking and how their minds might function.

How Does the Trauma Help?

The first way to reframe the trauma is to see what meaning one might have put into the trauma. The key is to ask a basic question: "Why this trauma is important and how it is impacting my life?" There are many possible answers to this. The trauma might have helped a person to reevaluate one's priorities. This includes developing a sudden revelation as to what is important to use in one's life in general. This trauma might also have created a change in one's mindset based on how much thinking was done to resolve certain problems caused by the trauma. New ways of thinking might have occurred with the possible goal of having corrected old and irrational ideas. An event may also make it easier for someone to have more confidence in other people. This could happen, as other people would be there to help someone deal with difficulties that have happened. Knowing how to resolve these problems will allow a person to be more comfortable with what is happening in their life.

Here's an example. John had become fearful and depressed following his father's death in a workplace accident. John experienced a great deal of trauma because his father was so important in his life. The trauma that John experienced might have caused him to think very differently about his priorities in his life and what he wants to do. He might have recognized that he needs to change some of the ways he gets along with people. This includes deciding to be with his family members more often and to stop being such a slave to his work. He would have made this decision with the knowledge that life is short and that he needs to be with those he cares for more often than he has in the past. Sometimes, knowing how to handle one's life and get through some of the more difficult situations can change how someone feels and what they think is important in life. The trauma in one's life can help a person to reorganize one's life and appreciate what they are thankful for.

How Cognitive Behavioral Therapy Controls Fears

The crippling effects and issues that can come with fears can prove to be difficult for anyone to live with. Once they have been identified, cognitive psychology can help control fears. As a person's fears are analyzed, their mental issues can be treated.

Realistic Thinking

One point of cognitive psychology in managing fears is thinking realistically. Sometimes, the fears a person exhibits might be based on outlandish or unrealistic beliefs. A person might be afraid of flying in an airplane because of the worry that the engines will stop working or something will break apart while in the air. A person has to think realistically. Because a person does not think realistically about what is involved, many fears develop. A person might not be aware that an airplane is durable and is constructed to stay intact in any conditions while in the air. Many people become afraid of flying because they do not understand how a plane works. Knowing the truth about something and what might happen can help alleviate fears. There are several steps that may be used to cognitively think about the problems that one has such as analyzing the certain issues surrounding a fear. Look for information relating to the item one is afraid of. Find connections between the fear and what can be done to resolve the issue. After looking at the connections, it becomes easier to understand the truth about what someone might be afraid of. This strategy is vital for people who have significant fears that are based on outlandish thinking. A person who is afraid of dogs out of the fear that they might attack will discover through training and analysis that any memories one might have had of dogs attacking could be based on unrealistic values or ideas and not reality.

Create Challenges to Negative Thoughts

Realistic thinking is helpful, but one way to go a step further is to produce cognitive challenges. Attempting to change your cognition over certain fears requires an effort to determine what one might be thinking at a certain time. There are a few steps that can be used to challenge some of the negative things that one might be thinking about.

- **Looking at the fortune-telling actions one engages in.**

    Many people link certain fears to the fortunes they tell themselves. A person might not want to touch a dog due to the belief that the dog will attack. The challenge, in this case, is to think about what will happen when someone pets a dog. When it is petted, the dog will probably not respond harshly. The dog will instead feel pleased and happy that someone is giving it attention. The fortune that someone told at the start might end up being false. By getting into a realistic situation with something, a person will discover that whatever was being done earlier is not something that someone has to be worried or fearful about.

- **Review over generalizations.**

    One part of improper cognitive thinking is people making generalizations. A person might have petted a dog and thinks that the rash they developed later was caused by that petting action. The truth is that the rash might have come from something else and not from the dog at all.

- **Think about the catastrophes that someone might consider possible.**

    When they overthink, catastrophes are problems that people get into. A person might think that when a person coughs while on an airplane that they might have some deadly or dangerous condition when most likely, they have allergies or a common cold.

- **Develop a plan to manage a fear.**

    Knowing what to do to control the fear is important. This can include having extra exposure to the stimuli that one is afraid of. Anyone who can handle a fear the right way will have a better chance at moving forward in life. When a person is ready to express your true self with a series of self-statements that are confident or positive in nature, often make fears easier to control.

- **Preparing self-statements.**

A person might say, "I am a smart person" or "I know what to do in certain situations that might happen." The process for producing self-statements and using them to manage the fears one holds will entail thinking about something positive in your life.

- **Review the cases where certain fears might happen.**

    Recall the positive self-statement that was produced. Make the statement relevant to the fear. Keep focusing on that statement and recognize how it applies to the fear. As the mind becomes more comfortable, the fear will be minimized. A good example of this is dealing with a fear of motorcycles. Because getting on one might be too risky, a person might be afraid of motorcycles. They might be afraid of slipping while on a motorcycle or something flying into your body and causing serious physical harm. A positive self-statement to use would be, "I am an alert person" or "I am very careful wherever I go." These statements reinforce the fact that there's nothing to be worried about and that he or she is careful. As the self-statement is repeated, the person who gets on the motorcycle will feel a little more comfortable. The positivity that comes from your mind will crowd out the negative thoughts. Once again, the statements can be remembered and restated whenever that person starts to feel nervous. After a while, the self-statements will not be necessary. The fear will not be as strong as the person will be used to the experience. In this situation, the person will know that the motorcycle one is on is much safer than what had been assumed it would have, been and they will no longer have that fear. The self-statements need to be realistic, relevant, and easy to recall.

Additional Questions to Ask

When considering the negative thoughts a person has that might cause a fear to develop, questions can be asked such as:

- **What evidence contradicts the thoughts one has?**

  This relates to realistic thinking. A person might say that he or she does not want to get on an airplane due to that plane being too dangerous. Evidence shows that millions of people fly on airplanes and there are thousands of flights that take off and land with no problems each day. Even personal evidence may be considered. A person might notice that your friends have gone on planes many times, and they did so safely.

- **What can be done to control any problems that might occur?**

    Many safeguards may be used to resolve any problems or worries one might have surrounding a fear. An airplane has many safety mechanisms that help to keep the vehicle operating in the air safely. Regular mandatory maintenance routines are also important to note. How long might it take for the fear in question to be fully resolved? People should not try to rush the process. It can take weeks or even months to conquer a fear, and it may never go away. The key is to allow the process of managing a fear or other worry to happen naturally. Asking enough questions about a fear helps to challenge the concerns that one has.

As a person's fears are analyzed, their mental issues can be treated. Sometimes, the fears a person exhibits might be based on outlandish or unrealistic beliefs. A person who is afraid of dogs out of the fear that they might attack will discover through training and analysis that any memories one might have had of dogs attacking could be based on unrealistic values or ideas and not reality.

Fears are often easier to control when a person is ready to express their true self with a series of self-statements that are confident or positive in nature. In this situation, the person will know that the motorcycle one is on is much safer than what had been assumed it would have been and they will no longer have that fear.

If you're enjoying this book, I would appreciate it if you went to the place of purchase and left a short positive review. Thank you.

Chapter 4 - Understanding Anxiety

Anxiety can be explained. Anxiety occurs where a person develops fears of failing or other problems. That person might have anxiety, as that person is worried that the email on the phone is from someone that the person is afraid of getting in touch with.

Anxiety is a feeling of worry or being uneasy about something that might develop in life. This includes worries about something that will happen in the future that a person is not fully certain or confident will actually happen. All people feel nervous at various points in their lives. Anxiety could develop into a state where it is hard for a person to maintain a good life. It is through the anxiety that a person will struggle to maintain a sense of peace due to the worries that are persistent. If managed by an appropriate plan, anxiety can be treated and resolved. Knowing how to control your sense of anxiety and worry in life can make a difference in what one wishes to do. It is through a general ability to manage anxiety that a person can have more control over your life and avoid having complicated issues. Anxiety occurs where a person develops fears of failing or other problems. The worries that someone has cannot be erased easily. The worries are constantly on the person's mind. The best way to explain anxiety is that it is like a fear that persists and is hard to control.

What Makes Fear and Anxiety Different?

Fear is uneasiness and worries about a very specific thing, whether it is an event, object, or person. Anxiety is more of a general feeling that persists that prevents a person from carrying on normal activities. A person might develop anxiety when reading your phone and noticing there is a symbol stating that someone has an email to read. That person might have anxiety, as that person is worried that the email on the phone is from someone that the person is afraid of getting in touch with. This is more pervasive than a basic fear due to the ongoing worries that someone might develop.

Common Worries of Anxious People

Anxiety is a problem that includes several common concerns. When they get into situations they are not comfortable with, it is natural for people to be worried or distressed. A person with an anxiety disorder will be much more anxious than what other people normally fear. Like with fears, the distress might be hard and very intense to cope with. Unlike fears, those worries could be very dramatic in many instances. Someone might be reluctant to get into certain situations. Sometimes, this will go into an outright refusal to do something. People who are anxious are very suspicious of what they might come across in life.

Some people might think about how entering one situation might be harmful or dangerous to them. There might be an ongoing fear of something traumatic happening in a situation. In the case of anxiety, this is more than just one specific stimulus. This may also involve multiple problems or concerns. The threats involved can be difficult and significant to bear. It might be difficult for a person to get to sleep due to the ongoing worries in your mind. Anxiety can cause a person to stop thinking about positive things and instead, concentrate on the negatives. An anxious person is not always going to openly declare certain feelings. Paying attention to physical symptoms associated with anxiety is very important. Cognitive Therapy may help you deal with all of these issues.

When someone is separated from another person, separation anxiety may occur. It is a condition where a person is worried about what might happen. A child might be anxious when they are apart from their parents. If they are separated for a period of time, a married couple could become anxious. Separation anxiety is more likely to occur in children. Those who have the closest relationships to another will feel the anxiety more severely. Separation anxiety is especially hard for people to resolve. Anxious feelings can last for weeks or months at a time, although it might be easier for a child to get over such a feeling.

The most common sign of a social anxiety disorder is when a person is trying to avoid certain situations, especially in public. There are two certain situations to notice. One is a person who might have a generalized fear. This comes across all the social situations someone experiences. The other is a specific fear that a social situation may also occur such as eating in public, talking to certain people in authority or control, and general public speaking situations. The fear involved might be based on your personal performance in a situation. This might include some thoughts that might be crippling and dangerous.

Generalized Anxiety Disorder

A generalized anxiety disorder focuses less on social situations and more about general events. This may be noticed based on how often a person might try to avoid entering into a situation. The symptoms that someone may have while in such a situation can be crippling due to that person feeling a lack of control and support. This problem may be linked up to nausea, diarrhea, or other physical issues that one might develop due to worry. General muscle pains may also develop in some of the worst situations. The threats can be dramatic and must be reviewed well to see what can come about in life and how different concerns might develop in general over what one wants to do.

Panic Disorder

A panic disorder is a condition where the feelings of panic will happen at random. This may occur even in cases where the situation seems relatively easy to control. A person with a panic disorder will feel anxiety at various times due to certain triggers. The panic that sets in can cause problems like sweating, a rapid heart rate, dizziness, and even general fears about a situation becoming worse. The damages of such an emotion can be potentially harmful and significant. A panic attack can last for a few minutes or might last for an hour.

Worries about Escape

There might be times where a person is afraid of being in a situation where they might not be able to get help or to escape. This concern is also known as agoraphobia. When worrying about your ability to escape a troubling or difficult situation, several things may be noticed. A person might be afraid of being on public transportation. That person has no control over the vehicle and might not get the help as needed. A person could also be afraid of open spaces where it is easy for that person to be targeted. These include parking lots and other spaces where it might be difficult for someone to get the help one needs. Enclosed spaces can be just as threatening to some people. These include spaces like theaters and shops. Being in a tight environment with lots of people can be just as threatening. When outside of the house alone, many might also be afraid of what one would do.

Sometimes a person might be quiet when approached with their worries or fears. This comes from what is known as selective mutism.

Selective mutism is easy to notice. It is a situation where a person is unable to speak in specific situations in life. This comes even though a person was unable to speak in particular situations elsewhere. A student might feel confident in your ability to talk to friends in many situations. That person might be vocal in the cafeteria at school or in a parking lot before or after class among other things. That same student might struggle to speak in other situations. They might not be able to deliver a presentation in class. That someone would freeze up and be unable to think about what to say. This could be due to a person struggling with situations where they do not have enough information. Maybe it is a situation that is formal. The condition is more common among people who might be new to a certain surrounding. Because they are unaware of what to do to handle a situation in the classroom, a new student at a school might be more likely to experience selective mutism. A new employee at a workplace might experience selective mutism due to being afraid of what other coworkers might think of them.

Post-Traumatic Stress Disorder

Post-Traumatic Stress Disorder or PTSD is a serious problem for some people. PTSD is a problem where a person experiences anxiety following a traumatic event. PTSD has been associated with people who have served in the military. They might have flashbacks to some of the things that they did or saw while in the field of war. PTSD is a problem that might come about for anyone. A person might also develop PTSD as a result of having an accident. This is especially the case for those in car wrecks as well as victims of assault which may include people who were subjected to sexual or child abuse. It may also be caused from suffering a disaster including man-made and natural disasters, experiencing a sudden event that caused death or another serious issue struggling with poverty or other financial traumas. The traumas can be often hard and significant to live with. It is through those traumas that a person might learn to be stronger and more capable of handling situations in life.

Dealing with Anxiety

Can a Single Plan Treat Any Kind of Anxiety?
It is true that anxiety can spread quickly in your mind and might not always be that easy to treat. It is critical for any person who struggles with anxiety to seek treatment. Every person who struggles with anxiety will respond to treatments uniquely and the treatments will vary.

Causes of Anxiety
Identifying the issues that cause anxiety is vital to helping people to get over their issues. Cognitive psychology suggests that when the issue is unraveled, it is easier for people to treat the condition.

Social Situations

Social situations can be difficult due to the fact that other people are involved and those people and their actions cannot be controlled. The problems could be significant and dramatic. A person might try to avoid certain social situations with the belief that those events would be dramatic and could add more triggers to your life than what one can handle at a moment.

Work Anxiety

Work anxiety can quickly occur at school or while on the job. A person might suffer from issues where one has to do something in public or get into a situation where your work is going to impact other people in some way. A student might have anxiety over being called upon by a teacher. Because they are unsure of what is required of them and they do not know how to communicate with other people in the classroom, that student might be afraid.

For work-related issues, a person might be afraid of what might happen when their boss wants to have a discussion. Because they are concerned or fearful about what might happen in the workplace, nervous feelings could develop.

Financial Worries

The financial stresses that someone might feel can surely cause. A person might be afraid of getting into a car wreck because they would be afraid of the monetary issues that will result. Even if your insurance was to cover everything and they were not going to actually lose money, they still might be anxious about the risk. The fact that the person might lose time at work or hours at school could make the situation problematic because they may fear what might happen if the injury or other issue caused by the accident were to be serious.

Traumatic Events

Post-Traumatic Stress Disorder or PTSD can be a significant problem that can influence anyone's life depends on how well your emotions are handled. The depth of anxiety will depend on the severity of the situation that someone might have experienced. People who suffer through traumatic events often try to keep the thoughts surrounding those events private. If they were open about the situations and the feelings they experience as a result of such events, they might be afraid of what people might think of them.

Control Anxiety by Tolerating Uncertainty

Having a plan to manage uncertainty is a part of CBT that assists people to replace the worries they have about unpredictability using some coping mechanisms. These mechanisms allow a person to know what to do when experiencing emotional stresses that occur when encountering a difficult situation.

Signs of Intolerance

A big part of anxiety is not being able to handle feelings of uncertainty and not knowing how to cope. Intolerance is an issue where a person is not willing to accept that a certain situation might or might not happen. An intolerant person is not ready to accept that some fear one has could be unlikely or unwarranted. Some of the things that an intolerant person might do include finding ways to avoid situations, delaying those situations so as not to have to deal with them or looking for reassurance to see that your beliefs or thoughts are fine but excessively checking something to see if it is false or true can be a problem. You may be doing this to skew the information to fit some your personal narrative.

Resolving Intolerance

The best thing that a person can do is to be ready to handle the uncertainty in your life. This can be accomplished by determining the specific behaviors one might engage in. Some of the behaviors that can be analyzed include things like seeking reassurance from other people, checking something regularly to get an idea of what is happening in a certain situation, or thinking too long before making a decision. Another example is a person who is trying to delay the decision-making process to avoid the consequences. Procrastinating or waiting until the last minute to do something is another way that intolerance can be manifested. Then there is simply actively avoiding a situation. Each of these signs suggests that a person might be struggling to respond and feel comfortable with a situation. Look at the situation that has been presented and think about the possible outcomes. People who are anxious often assume that very specific outcomes might occur. By considering at all the different outcomes, it becomes easier for someone to find an answer about dealing with the certain situation. Look at the anxious thoughts and consider how realistic or outlandish some of the thoughts might be. Rank all the problems according to the amount of anxiety that is produced. Some people might feel worried about responsibilities or tasks or even with everyday routines. Make a list of what can be controlled versus what cannot.

Avoidance Coping

Avoidance coping is a problem that often comes as a result of uncertainty intolerance.This is a situation

where a person will try to avoid situations that they are unable to control or predict. This form of coping is often a threat that makes life restricted. The main reason a person engages in avoidance coping is that the person feels that something negative might happen. There might be some improper comparisons that the person is making.

These include situations where a person assumes that one problem will come about following a certain action. Because there are too many things that might go wrong, the person will be conditioned to assume that nothing good is going to happen.

Cognitive psychology suggests that those who understand what they can and cannot do will be more likely to feel at peace. This helps people to make more rational decisions as they understand that there are rules as to what they can and cannot do. It is best to be open to accepting all the things that could occur and creating a smart plan for handling issues.

Preparation

While the process of cognitive diffusion can work, it is even better when the right preparations are considered. The following efforts for preparation may be used to keep the situation under control. Determine the situations in which negative thoughts are likely to take place. Consider possible replacement thoughts about a situation. Review the realistic nature of the situations. Look at the situations one might encounter. Is there some kind of trigger point or other feature in a situation that might make it hard to do? When keeping a thought realistic, you can come up with real solutions to your problems.

Cognitive Diffusion to Control anxiety

There are many techniques that can help manage anxiety, but one of the most important ones is cognitive diffusion. When a person is removed from your thoughts, this is a process. People are often so attached to their thoughts that it becomes next to impossible to resolve worries or fears that might develop. Cognitive diffusion is the opposite of cognitive fusion. In the case of fusion, a person will believe that all of your thoughts are true and accurate. Cognitive diffusion is where a person will acknowledge thoughts as basic thoughts. That is, they know that their thoughts are not necessarily true. They are just thoughts that come along as they are. There is no need to believe or disbelieve any of them. That each thought should be looked at to discern the truth in it. Cognitive diffusion can work for any negative thoughts that one has.

When Does Cognitive Diffusion Work?

Cognitive diffusion is a part of cognitive therapy that may work in situations like when someone is feeling negative about the thoughts that they are having and where the thoughts are too depressing or are making your work harder to manage. Someone who has a low self-esteem could use cognitive diffusion to reorganize their thoughts and treat them differently. People who worry too much and need to remove the emotions to keep worries from being too intense.

Those who suffer from OCD-related anxiety or fears can benefit as diffusion. It can reduce the intensity of compulsive thoughts. Those who might be living in the past and are playing the same memories or thoughts several times over need cognitive diffusion to lessen the intensity of those thoughts.

How to Use Cognitive Diffusion

The following steps can be used to keep the problems of difficult thoughts from being more of a burden than necessary. The first step is to acknowledge the thought, no matter what it might be. Spend some time interpreting the meaning of the thought. This helps to create a sense of clarity. At this point, you have accepted and tried to understand your repeating thoughts. This is a big step that will lead you to eventually let go of the memory as long as you put the work in. The thought does not have to be acknowledged for too long. Sometimes, just considering the thought for a few seconds is good enough.

Change the Focus

Do not continue focusing on a thought or issue. It helps to go into another room or area or maybe even change whatever action someone is doing. This keeps the original thought that came about from being too intense. Pay attention to something different without necessarily passing judgment on the thought that just occurred. The focus does not have to be on something relating to the same topic either. The new topic can be radically different from what one was thinking about earlier. The only need is to change the thoughts and feelings one has before they can become harder to deal with.

Observe the Issue

After the focus is changed, the intensity of the thought is slightly weakened. An observation like "I am thinking about..." is often good enough. This is enough to acknowledge the presence without the thought of becoming intense and the feelings of anxiety need to be curbed.

Planning for cognitive diffusion is needed for getting more out of your work. Knowing how to manage certain thoughts the right way and how to keep those worries from being a burden should help anyone to succeed and grow.

Recognizing Intrusive Memories

Many of the memories you will have is related to the events that took place in your life. These events, as mentioned earlier, are episodic memories. They can be detailed, and they are often biographical in nature. Those memories are usually positive and can be recalled as pleasant. Some of the memories people might experience include those that are difficult and, in some cases, make the anxiety feel worse. These memories are called intrusive memories. Jeff might have memories relating to his days in high school. He felt happy being with his friends and learned some great things from many teachers who were happy and helpful. He might recall negative moments as well. Jeff might recall an event that was not pleasant such as a car accident while driving to school. Because he was too nervous, perhaps he has a memory of trying to give a presentation but failing. Those negative memories will cause him to feel anxious.

Once again, about not doing well in a social situation or maybe getting into another accident in his car, he might begin to worry. In this situation, Jeff had some intrusive memories that got in the way of the good ones. These were hidden in his mind for a while. He might not have been aware that he had those memories until they surfaced.

Characteristics of Intrusive Memories

Intrusive memories can be about anything that might have happened in your life. There are some types of intrusive memories that might be more prominent than others. Here are a few of the general characteristics of intrusive memories.

Intrusive memories are triggered without warning. When a person thinks of something, an intrusive memory will almost surely happen and trigger your anxiety further. Then the memory returns. When a memory like this happens, it becomes easy for someone to be worried or confused. The intrusive memory will develop due to a person having a memory that links directly to the old one. In Jeff's case, the memory of a car accident returned as he was thinking about hanging out with his friends. The relationship of his high school days to that particular event is very close. The intrusive memory can be vivid. Many intrusive memories can be intense and more detailed than others. Part of this is due to the negative imagery and feelings that the memory produced. For Jeff, the imagery that comes with the car accident could be vivid. When he wasn't hurt, he might recall the sound of his car getting hit or the panic he felt afterward. The worries that he had were intense, and they left an impact on him. The vivid nature of his memory makes it feel as though he is reliving that moment in time. The memory could be about any event, but in most cases, it involves a traumatic event. One of the greatest problems with life is that the positive memories are always fleeting, and yet the negative memories will persist. Those memories are ones that cause a person to feel a sense of panic and dread. A person who has regular anxiety issues might suffer from regular flashbacks. This is especially the case for those who have PTSD and cannot stop reliving certain traumatic events in their lives. When a flashback occurs, someone will have a feeling that the trauma that one experienced in the past is actively happening again. All the pressure and stress that one experienced will return. The emotional and mental anxiety and feelings that occurred at the time will return and disrupt all other feelings and make concentration difficult.

Chapter 5 - Stoicism and CBT

Stoicism is a philosophy that stretches back to ancient Greece. Stoicism is an "operating system" for leading a better life. Stoicism holds that a virtuous life is a good life and offers principles of virtuous behavior based on generations of observation and trial and error. Stoicism is also about accepting fate, reality, or the "laws of the universe," including factors beyond the perceptions of our minds. Stoicism asserts that reason is our human connection to these laws. Therefore, we must use reason independently of the likes and dislikes, pain and pleasure, and everyday desires and worries. Stoicism encourages rational thinking, self-awareness, and practical wisdom and teaches that we should avoid being overly attached to certain outcomes or desires. It teaches us to be aware of our stream-of-consciousness thoughts and to be slow to accept and emotionally react to them. As with CBT, the idea is that unchecked automatic thoughts can cause negative emotions, so we should carefully examine thoughts before reacting emotionally. The general strategy of ancient Stoicism is, once a thought has been identified, to evaluate whether it relates to something that is under your control. If not, the thought should be let go. Stoics believe that tranquility can be achieved by developing a clear understanding of what is under our control (our minds) and what is not (everything else), and then fully accepting that reality and what results from it.

A Latin phrase, amor fati (a love of fate), became popular among Stoic practitioners, who reasoned that what must be accepted may as well be embraced lovingly. They argued that confusion about what we have influence over is a cause of suffering. Just as fish have minimal influence in the ocean, we humans have only minimal influence in the universe. This is not to say we have no power; rather, we should focus our efforts inward, toward our own minds and attitudes. Not doing so leads to pointless struggle and suffering. CBT borrows from Stoicism in three fundamental areas: logic, acceptance, and right action.

Let's look at these in more detail. Logic, according to Stoics, is the filter that separates the wise from the unwise. We often see things as we imagine them to be rather than how they really are. The truth becomes distorted by dysfunctional cognitive frameworks, resulting in destructive emotions and suffering. This gap between perception and reality can be distinguished only by logic. Logic dictates that rather than attempting to change nature, you need to change your thoughts to align with reality. The more you're successful at doing this, the more you'll be able to fill the gaps, and the less you'll suffer. Accepting nature—with all its ups and downs and good and bad—is the second key tenet of Stoicism. This reflects a duality taught by many religions: For every light, there's darkness; for every pleasure, there's pain. Suffering, agony, and death are as much part of the natural law as happiness, pleasure, and birth all occurring in turn. There's beauty in this world, and there's terror too. Accept both for a balanced, contented life.

This does not mean that Stoicism enables passivity and fatalism. Stoicism encourages right action—the third tenet—when possible and accepts inaction only when the outcomes are not within human control. This concept is echoed in the famous Serenity Prayer written by American theologian Reinhold Niebuhr: *Grant me the serenity to accept the things I cannot change, courage to change the things I can, and the wisdom to know the difference.* The third tenet of right action is based on the teaching that we cannot change what happens to us but we can change how we respond. If someone insults us in public, there's nothing we can do to change that fact after it has occurred, but we can control how we react. Stoics believe that rather than waste energy on trying to control external circumstances, we should spend that same energy on controlling our responses to those circumstances in a positive way. This eventually helps to change the world—one individual at a time—and even could assist in controlling the circumstances that caused this change in the first place. Stoicism also encourages taking actions that promote well-being and avoiding those that harm it.

Negative Visualization

One particular Stoic technique that fits well with CBT is negative visualization. Negative visualization is based on the idea that imagining possible or inevitable negative events ahead of time prepares us for their possible occurrence. As a result, they will be less shocking, and we will be better equipped to either prevent them or deal with them. Negative visualization can help address some types of intrusive thoughts, especially worry intrusions. Negative visualization dates back to the Roman Stoic philosophers Seneca and Epictetus. Before taking a trip, for example, Seneca would imagine everything that could possibly go wrong, and adjust his plans so he could avoid or deal with the bad possibilities. Think of this part as a practical exercise. In the situation that is causing you stress or generating intrusive worry thoughts, logically go through the series of events and assess where problems could occur.

In some cases, you may realize that things you are worried about are extremely unlikely to occur, or downright impossible. That can help put your mind at ease. For other possibilities, make a plan. Taking preventive action can help address unproductive anxiety. Negative visualization can also be used to help us value what we have, by imagining our lives without it. This can be useful even when we are unlikely to lose something. For example, married couples might grow accustomed to each other over time, some to the point that they forget how important they are to each other and take the other's presence for granted. This could lead one or both of them to treat the other with indifference or contempt, to ignore each other, or even to do things that are incredibly hurtful, like beginning an affair with a new partner.

Stoic philosophers believe that this attitude can be prevented by frequently imagining life without one's spouse. Even though it can feel upsetting, a husband or wife who imagines life without the other each morning is likely to be more appreciative, grateful, and loving. It can prompt them to make better use of the time they have together, such that they are less likely to separate and that when one does die, the other can grieve without feeling regret. You can try it with anything in your life that you want to value more—a parent, partner, or child; your health, your home, or your ability to work; or living in a safe neighborhood or a country with political freedoms. Imagine in detail your life without that thing. Would it be harder? Less joyful? Lonelier? Less meaningful? Think about it and then be sure to translate that newfound appreciation into action.

Tell your loved ones how important they are to you. Be active while you are in good health. Be grateful for your job. Exercise your free speech. This simple exercise can make the things you already have feel like a lot more. In some cases, people suffer from anxiety related to the loss of these same types of things, but without the second key part of negative visualization: taking action. This exercise is pointless if you just create feelings of distress and sadness. You must find a way to use the negative energy of anxiety to push you forward into positive action. This way, if you do lose one of the valuable parts of your life, you will not feel that you wasted the time you had with it. We may encounter another type of event, one that is sad or difficult and will inevitably happen. For example, most of us will experience the death of a parent at some point. It could also be a loved one with a terminal illness or a beloved pet with a life-span naturally much shorter than our own. It could also be something like our children growing up and leaving to start their own lives.

For many people, these thoughts are quite distressing and may be the basis of anxiety-related intrusive thoughts. Negative visualization encourages us to imagine these situations, as sad as they may be. Seneca, one of the ancient developers of Stoic thought, explained that "we should love all our dear ones... but always with the thought that we have no promise that we may keep them forever—nay, no promise even that we may keep them for long." Negative visualization can thus help us realize that loss is a part of life and can prepare us for it so that we will, eventually, be OK. Perhaps life won't ever be the same, perhaps it will be harder, and perhaps it will be even better after a while, but we will find a way to continue. In ancient times, in the absence of therapists and psychiatrists, philosophers acted as "physicians of the soul," and people turned to them for guidance. Stoicism was considered a powerful tool for mental well-being, especially in the Hellenic period, and philosophy was a necessity as counseling is today. It was accessible to everyone, and contrary to the perceptions of philosophy today, it was not about abstract wisdom. Stoicism offered simple, everyday solutions for everyday problems, and the practical concepts are popular to this day. In ancient Greece, it was normal to seek help from a philosopher for mental health issues.

Mental illnesses require remedies like any other, and ancient societies understood this better than we do. As we borrow their wisdom, we also need to embrace their sensibilities and worldview when it comes to the malady and its treatment. Given the similarity of CBT to Stoic philosophy, you could think of contemporary therapists as a type of philosopher, helping people understand themselves and the world around them in more realistic and effective ways. In this respect, their role hasn't changed much since the days of ancient Greece. The Greeks were concerned as much with the world as with the individual and how they related to each other. Today's cognitive behavioral therapists are part of that long legacy, helping to create harmony within the human mind in relation to the world. Of course, therapy has evolved over time, but its fundamentals have remained strikingly similar to ancient wisdom.

Chapter 6 - Mindfulness Is Vital

A patient in a CBT procedure must know about the issues one is battling with. This incorporates investigating what emotions they may have. These sentiments may seem impossible to identify, but they aren't. A person's line of reasoning ought to be investigated and whether it may be tied by specific feelings. The issues that somebody experiences may be a risk to their prosperity. The most serious issue with this is that it is difficult to make sense of to what extent it will take to have more authority over your life. There is no real way to tell when a time of mindfulness starts and when it ends. As the feelings and contemplations are watched, a person will begin to understand a portion of the issues one is going through. Sometimes, this may require a second individual to call attention to out specific issues.

This could mean letting someone know when they are exhibiting negative thoughts and actions. Mindfulness can help an individual who needs assistance the most. It will help a person understand exactly what is required for progress. It is through this freshly discovered learning that a person will begin to move in the direction that will end up changing your life around and settling the enormous stresses that one has created. Having more authority over your psyche is essential for the accomplishment of the job that needs to be done.

As one begins to be more mindful of the sentiments and feelings they have, it is evident that there are both positive and negative emotions and triggers are the reason for these emotions. As troublesome as it may be for individuals to consider, the negative things that somebody is thinking must be investigated and checked on with care. By distinguishing the negative thoughts one has, it winds up simpler to recognize the issues that are causing the negative or unforgiving considerations. Negative conduct reactions, physical issues, and different stresses can make things harder for some to deal with. The reactions that one has to specific ideas or thoughts must be investigated all the while.

To get a thought of how this works, let's look at an example. Suppose that Mark is endeavoring to deal with his general anxiety related to his working life. He may have a critical mental hang-up where he always gets anxious when he sees that his cell phone has a text notification. He may be worried about the possibility that the individual who is reaching him may be furious. He would state that he is concerned that the text notification would be from his manager. He says this on the grounds that there have been times in the past where his boss has sent furious text messages about how he isn't getting his work done right. Mark would end up anxious when he sees that little symbol on his telephone revealing to him that a text is waiting for him on his phone. However, by and large, that content isn't what he supposes it would be. Or maybe, it could be a message from another person or a constructive message from his boss. Mark would use CBT to enable him to control and assuage his tension so he won't feel along these lines when he takes a look at his telephone and sees that marker. In this circumstance, he would need to survey his stress over the telephone notifications. He needs to examine the issue with somebody who can encourage him. He, at that point, needs to build up a relationship with the individual who could help him. The therapist ought to be of solace and support to him. The relationship might be with an expert specialist, albeit in some cases, working closely with a companion can be similarly as useful. The uneasiness must be investigated in detail. The considerations can be broken down in view of how they have affected his life.

A survey of the past has to be considered. Mark must be made mindful of what he is doing. Now and again, his brain may be blurred with the goal that he doesn't comprehend what he is doing, hence making him act nonsensically. As Mark becomes mindful, he feels a sudden need to determine the issues. This prompts a survey of the negative sentiments he has. Everything that he knew about must be investigated in view of how positive the circumstance may be. The reshaping procedure can start at this crossroads. Mark will work with an expert to enable him to reshape his considerations and find better approaches to control his tension. This incorporates figuring out how to maintain a strategic distance from the stressed sentiments that he creates when he sees that content warning. He may, likewise, figure out how to supplant those stressed thoughts or how to take part in activities that is a portion of the inadequacies in his manners of thinking. As Mark takes these suggestions, he will have more power over his life and how he will lead it. He will begin to see that there is no purpose behind his tension over that message. Having the assistance that he needs will guarantee that he can keep from being anxious or stressed.

Mindfulness is often incorporated into cognitive therapy processes as a means of getting away from negative thought patterns including those that can cause a person to develop anxiety and struggle to manage the situation. Mindfulness is a practice that focuses on helping a person to relax and be at ease with their self. The effort involves physical efforts to keep positive and calm and give someone the power needed to keep your mind from being overburdened by difficult problems that may develop. A person who is mindful will have an easier time handling your worries and feelings. Keeping those problems in control makes it easier for someone to feel positive and relaxed with what one wants to do. There are several positive things that come from being mindful. The ruminations that someone has will become less pervasive or frequent. This reduces the risk of negative thoughts to occur or for one to focus too much on the same things or issues. When they are ready and mindful to handle the subject matter, it becomes easier for people to face their issues and problems. When the right plans for handling life are managed, people can also make better and smarter choices. When finding a way to become happier and in control, mindfulness is a necessity for people to follow. The steps for being mindful are thinking about what is happening in your mind. Knowing how to manage certain problems that might develop and to keep them from being so strong is vital to your success. Sensory information should be reviewed alongside points on how easy it is for tasks to be finished. Relax for a few minutes each day. Take time to relax for a bit each day. People can do anything they want to relax.

Meditation helps people to focus their thoughts on certain things and to learn how to concentrate. You can use aromatherapy oils in a diffuser in your room. The relaxing scents might help to clear your thoughts. Go to a quiet room and think about what has gone on throughout the day. Consider how certain events occurred through the actions that took place in the day. Take calming and deep breaths regularly. Keeping your breath in check makes it easier for someone to feel rested and relaxed. Any of these practices can work in any situation. Recognize certain feelings as they occur. Consider some of the feelings that were produced during the day and what caused those feelings to come about. How did they go away? These points should be explored to figure out what causes those feelings to grow and become intense in some situations. Have more breaks during the day. It is understandable why people might try to do as much work as they can.

People might work ten or twelve or even fifteen hours a day at times. Because they feel they need more money or they are afraid of letting people down by saying no to certain tasks, they might do so. All that work can become problematic. It becomes easier for a person to become stressed. This causes a person to feel worried and anxious. Adding breaks during the day helps a person feel more comfortable with your work. Those who relax and take breaks regularly will not be likely to make errors while on the job. Always acknowledge the progress one makes. Being able to recognize the progress to complete a task is vital for success. This gives a clear idea of what someone is doing and how well the efforts one has put in are working. Be kind about any criticism. Sometimes, criticism is warranted.

Cognitive psychology suggests that those who link faults and other issues to positive thoughts will have an easier time moving forward in life. It helps to be positive about any faults that one has. The happiest people who feel no anxiety are those who accept themselves for who they are and are not afraid to accept criticism. Criticisms help people to find new things that they can do to grow their lives and feel stronger about who they are. Each of these steps for mindfulness will go a long way toward handling your anxiety. Mindfulness is an aspect of cognitive psychology that lets people link what they are thinking to their actions, thus making their work more valuable.

Ideas for Mindfulness

There are several exercises can be used to help people become mindful and in control. The goal of these exercises is to think about something that causes anxiety or another negative feeling and to let that problem go by the wayside. Getting rid of the burden that comes along is needed for preventing significant problems to get worse and otherwise be a challenge. In your mind, spray paint a thought onto a vehicle like a train, car, or van. Watch that vehicle move down  the road or railway to watch it disappear. This exercise lets a person notice some of the worries or emotional problems disappear. Watch a thought as it appears on a billboard on the road. Imagine driving past that billboard or going through a tunnel that keeps the billboard from being visible. Watch as the clouds form in the sky and see how they disappear after a while.

Imagine your thoughts as those clouds. Look as they appear and eventually disappear. Look how a stream flows along and the water moves by. See any natural items that might be flowing along with the water. These might represent the thoughts one has. These can flow by and keep your mind from having the same thoughts all the time. Just knowing how to visualize these thoughts as they move away and stop bothering your mind is often good enough for keeping issues from being too pervasive.

How Long Does Mindfulness Take?

Mindfulness is a practice that requires a bit of training. People can spend as much time as they want to manage their emotions and to use mindfulness to make their train of thought easier to handle. Expect to spend a bit of extra time trying to handle your feelings of mindfulness to calm anxiety. After the issue disappears, it should become a little easier for problems to be resolved. The physical effects of mindfulness should help a person rest and feel relaxed. The body will still feel alert regarding other things. The mindful feelings that someone develops could help to relax the mind and, therefore, keep the body from having an increase in blood pressure rate or heart rate. It is through the amygdala that the body is capable of handling the stresses or worries that one has.

Can Mindfulness Occur Right After a Triggering Situation?

Because the mental and emotional pressures they are in are too strong, those who have triggering events in their lives might feel as though they cannot do more for themselves. Mindfulness-related practices can be used at any time of the day and in any place. Remember that mindfulness is designed to work to keep the thoughts one has and the feelings or issues under control. This helps to prevent certain problems relating to your thoughts from being difficult and pervasive.

Progressive Muscle Relaxation

Another part of cognitive behavioral therapy that relates to being mindful involves the use of progressive muscle relaxation. Knowing how to manage your muscles and to keep them from feeling stressed is vital for your success. As a person becomes fearful or anxious, the muscles start to become tense. Progressive muscle relaxation helps to keep those physical stresses under control. The main purpose of PMR is to rest the muscles in two key steps. Specific muscles will be targeted. All the tension that was produced from stress and anxiety can be released. PMR helps people reduce the effects of headaches, stomachaches, and the ongoing desire to dwell on a negative thought. As the stresses are removed, the mind will be more productive and emotionally organized. When the muscles are relaxed, there is also a potential for the body to get to sleep quicker. Progressive muscle relaxation is great for managing the physical issues of anxiety. When they have worrying feelings that trigger anxiety, PMR helps people establish cues for what they can do. It is easier to feel confident when the body is relaxed, refreshed, and comfortable.

You will notice when your body starts to get tense, thus helping you come up with a plan for resolving the issue via PMR. The steps to practice the PMR require some preparation at the start.

1. Find a calm and quiet place to practice this for at least 15 minutes.
2. Add tension to a small part of your body at the beginning. For example, some tension can be applied onto your shoulders by having the hands grab onto the shoulders and squeeze lightly.
3. Do this for about five seconds to allow the muscles to feel the added pressure. Wait for a few seconds and then release the tension that was added to the muscle.
4. Exhale and let out all the tension that was produced. Focus on how the tension disappears. Recognize the release.
5. Stay in a relaxed state for a few moments.
6. It only takes about 15 seconds for the body to feel rested. Do not try to rush the

process. Focus on the tension as it is released.

7. Move on to the next part of the body that might be experiencing stress. Allow the stresses to be released without adding lots of pressure.

When doing this, it becomes easier for the body to release all the stresses. Be careful and cautious. While this takes place, visualize something positive while relieving your tensions. Whatever is being visualized can be used to help keep the mind from feeling lots of pressure or worry. The new image linked to the process can be brought up in your mind while relaxing. As the positive image comes up in your mind, it becomes easier for a person to release the pressure of stress they have been bottling up. Getting enough practice helps anyone managing PMR becomes second nature after a while. When someone is not actually feeling any anxiety, this practice can still be used.

How is the Body Targeted?

This muscle relaxation process works best when the body is targeted in this order. Start with the foot and leg area. The lower parts of the body are to be targeted first as this is believed to be where the energy starts. Some argue that the feet are the key parts of the body that can benefit the most from relaxation therapy. Then target the stomach and chest. Finally, go with the arm and hand area. You can simply stretch the other parts of the body outward like the neck and shoulders. A mix of both stretching and massaging can be very helpful. Don't neglect the various areas around the head; opening your mouth wide, clenching the eyelids shut, and raising your eyebrows up high along the forehead. As the process of relaxation continues, it should become a little easier for people to feel comfortable and in check with their bodies.

Chapter 7 - CBT and Depression

Aperson who suffers from depression experiences negative feelings which can become pervasive to the point where it is next to impossible for a person to do the things one wants to do in life. The family members of those who suffered from depression are more likely to experience depression themselves.

The Depression Cycle

To fully understand what makes depression hard to live with, it is important to look at how the depression cycle works.

Common Effects to Watch For

To treat someone who is suffering from depression, it is vital to look at the effects of the depression. Depression is often seen as a lifelong issue that will change things in your life and make it harder for a person to carry and think on normally.

Depression is one of the most misunderstood mental disorders. This is a problem that can be serious and can lead to self-harm and isolation. Depression has been closely linked to suicidal thoughts or actions. To outsiders, depression appears to be a condition where someone just feels tired and lonely most of the time. For those who really suffer this kind of mental health issue, they find it hard to have the energy of motivation to even do menial tasks, more so for other tasks or activities that can help them to experience life and its happiness. Cognitive behavioral therapy may work to help control depression and to help a person feel more positive about life. Because depression is hard to figure out and control, this would require an immense amount of support and assistance. When managed appropriately, the risk of harmful behaviors as a result of your depression can be reduced.

What Causes Depression?

Depression is a problem that involves a person feeling unhappy or hopeless for an extensive amount of time. The situation causes a person to feel as though nothing good is going to happen and nothing is going to change that. The emotional burden is a problem, but it is also a condition that many people are not fully aware of. Many do not understand what causes depression. Genetics may cause depression to develop in some people. Those who have family members who suffered from depression are more likely to experience depression themselves. It is not fully clear as to why genetics play such a role in depression. Searching up online and one can find numerous studies and researches that centers on genetics and depression.

The Brain

The brain could be a factor as to why depression might develop in your mind. The neurotransmitters in your brain might become unbalanced. This is especially the case with dopamine, a transmitter that regulates feelings of happiness. This often leads to people to use medications to control feelings of depression. Some medications are used to temporarily resolve depressed feelings. They are not necessarily going to treat the deeper cause of the depression.

Hormonal Changes

As the body's hormones change, it becomes harder for a person to manage your emotions. The emotional impact of hormonal changes makes it harder for a person to have healthy emotions. This, in turn, keeps the mind from being in control. Women are often more likely to develop depression as a result of hormonal changes. The impacts of such changes during menopause can be often hard and dramatic for many women to adjust.

Seasonal Affective Disorder

Seasonal Affective Disorder, or SAD, is a condition where a person experiences a disturbance in sleeping habits when the days are shorter and the night much longer. This often occurs during the winter season. This change in light impacts the natural rhythms of the body. A person can experience persistent and sudden fatigue. SAD is not something that all people will experience. However, it can be a threat to some. Because they are unavoidable and often entail regular routines being dramatically disrupted, the problems that occur due to SAD can be hard and dramatic for some people to live through. SAD can also worsen when a person doesn't get in touch with their family more often and find the winter season more isolating. People who live in colder climates where the days are shorter are typically more likely to suffer from SAD-related problems.

Stresses in Life

Sometimes, the immense stresses that people might experience can become too hard for them to live with. Those stresses can make life difficult. It is widely believed that the hormonal changes that occur during high-stress situations might be a factor in what causes a person to change behaviors or attitudes. When the body feels stress, cortisol is produced. This hormone can influence how serotonin, dopamine, and other hormones are produced. The imbalance in brain chemicals can cause a person's natural brain functions to stop working accordingly. This, in turn, increases the likelihood for someone to develop depression.

Moments of Grief

Intense feelings of grief that someone might experience can become significant and serious, such as grief from traumatic events and especially from the loss of a loved one. The lack of a desire to do normal tasks following a significant loss will only make your life harder. The specific causes of your depression will vary for each person. Understanding what may cause someone to experience depression may help with determining what can be done to help that person.

The Depression Cycle
To fully understand what makes depression hard to live with, it is important to look at how the depression cycle works. In the beginning, a person will suffer from a lack of energy. The lack of energy does not have to just be physical fatigue. It could be as simple as struggling to have interest or enthusiasm. A person might be bored with the same job or routine done every day. Repeating the same tasks, again and again, will

disinterest a person and lose their energy to even help themselves enjoy just a bit away from their everyday routine.

The Beginnings of Neglect

A depressed person will start to do fewer things, will stop following regular routines, and accept normal responsibilities. The guilt will increase. It becomes easier for someone to feel unhappy and guilty with their life because of the neglect and lack of interest. They will feel ineffective and hopeless in life due to how one is unable to take or complete certain jobs part in regular activities. The human mind will feel positive and tired thoughts will be elusive. The lack of work, activity, and inability to move will lead to intense depression. The problem will get worse as it continues. The cycle will start all over again. Those negative feelings will lead to a further loss of interest. The worst part of the cycle of depression is that it will continue and become more severe the longer the cycle persists.

Common Symptoms to Watch For

To treat someone who is suffering from depression, it is vital to look at the symptoms of the depression. These problems are among the more common concerns to watch for:

- ***A person's mood might change***.
  Other people will notice and say that you've become lonelier and lifeless. They will wonder why you've suddenly changed

into that kind of personality when they have known you for being a happy person.

- ***A person might be struggling to stay interested in some of the things that a person would normally be interested in***.
They would show a lack of interest on the things they love to do, their habits, their ambitions, the things that they admire, and much more. Their interest in a specific thing can be measured based on how much enthusiasm they show towards that thing.

- ***There might be noticeable changes in your weight.***
People who are depressed are more likely to either gain or lose weight even though they do not intend to. A person might gain weight from eating to feel better. Someone might also lose weight due to a lack of interest in food.

- ***Someone might experience dramatic changes in sleeping habits.***

Some of the more common changes in sleep are either sleeping too much or not getting to sleep at all. A person might feel tired even after waking up or tired at various points throughout the day.

- ***There could be a lack of the ability to concentrate.***
  Because they lack the interest to stay involved, those who are frequently depressed might not know how to concentrate or make decisions.

- ***The worst situations are people who might regularly think about death or self-harm.***
  It is natural for people to be afraid of death, but a depressed person will have a greater focus on the possibility of death. The added preoccupation that someone has toward death could be a sign that someone is willing to cause themselves harm.

What Are the Long-Term Effects?

If the concern is not managed properly, the worst part about depression is that it can become extremely serious. Depression can be devastating as the issue makes someone feel worried or panicked about life. Depression makes it harder for a person to do anything. It keeps people from feeling comfortable around others. Because a person might be isolating themselves from others, relationships and friendships can be affected. Depression is a mental concern that may lead people into harming themselves. Because a person might feel unhappy with their life and thinks that things will not get any better no matter how they try or no matter what happens, these can often lead to worst situations like having suicidal thoughts and actions.

Men and Women

Women are often more likely to experience depression than men. The main reason for this is how they respond to depressing events or other things that are too hard. When a man comes across a problem in his life, he is more likely to distract himself. He might struggle to deflect his attention from a problem, thus making it easier for him to be hard and judgmental on himself. A woman would be more likely to ruminate about what she is experiencing. She will think about the problems and how it is keeping her from feeling happy. That burden will make it harder for her to concentrate and enjoy activities. This does not mean that men are not likely to ruminate about things, nor does it mean women are not going to try to distract themselves from the issues they encounter.

Can Depression Be Cured?

Depression is often seen as a lifelong issue that will change things in your life and make it harder for a person to carry and think on normally. Depression makes it hard for people to live healthy lives and to think straight all the time. It is through the work provided by CBT that the effects of depression and the emotional worries that are produced by this condition can be resolved. Depression is a very dramatic problem that must be controlled. Cognitive psychological ideas might help in resolving the situation.

If you're enjoying this book, I would appreciate it if you went to the place of purchase and left a short positive review. Thank you.

Chapter 8 - Anger and How CBT Corrects the Situation

Anger is a problem that many people feel at times and is also a concern that makes it harder for a person to get along with other people. It is an emotion that everyone is bound to feel at some point. Anger can be triggered by just about anything. The anger someone holds might be due to something that didn't go as how the person thought and planned to happen. It may also come from envy when a person doesn't receive the same amount or kind of things, treatment, and positivity that another person has. Anger is a concern that can permeate your life and trigger feelings of frustration. It is critical for people to understand what they can do to handle certain problems relating to anger.

Recognizing the Body's Response to Anger

Anger is a problem that will cause the body to respond in a unique fashion. Some of the things that will happen within the body include the following:

- An angry person's body will start to release adrenaline. This is a hormone that causes muscles to tighten while the heart rate increases.

- The amygdala in the brain will be triggered to cause significant frustrations and anger in your mind.

- The body's senses might become more sensitive. They will be more likely to notice some of the unpleasant things and triggers.

- The skin may also appear flushed, although this is primarily due to the increased heart rate and body temperature that accompanies anger.

The frustration that comes with anger can be dramatic. It is through your ability to handle anger that it might be easier for a situation to be resolved. Knowing what causes anger can be significant.

What Causes Anger?

Anger is a frustrating feeling, but it is something that must be explored to understand it. There are many things that might cause anger. Certain triggers in your mind can cause someone to feel angry. These include triggers that focus on things one does not like. Situations, where something does not go a person's way, can be upsetting. In many cases, a trigger might develop when someone makes a plan for the day but ends up losing control of those plans. Traumatic memories may also be a trigger. There are, oftentimes, when outside sources might cause someone to become angry and incapable of controlling their mind. Your individual history can contribute to feelings of anger. The past events or the biases or attitudes one holds might cause anger to become worse. The threat of anger is significant in that a person who becomes angry will be harder to communicate and manage with.

Acknowledging the Anger

There are many things that can be done using CBT. Anyone who keeps their anger bottled up might struggle with keeping their body under control. The pains and sensations that someone might feel may become worse and harder to control when anger comes into your mind. Suppressing anger is only going to make the situation more difficult. How can the anger be expressed without taking it out on someone? The best thing to do is to recognize the anger and notice that the feeling is developing. Be aware of the angry situation and make some self-statements that recognize what is happening. An angry person might say something like, "My heart rate is starting to go up" or "Whatever is going on here is not what I intended to have happened." Be willing to address the anger, but do not project the anger outward toward other people. Having a sense of control over how the anger is handled will help anyone to manage your mind. Considering the anger in question and acknowledging its presence can go a long way toward helping a person manage the issues that caused the anger.

Review the Anger

After acknowledging the anger directly, it is time to review that anger. Look at the issue that caused the anger to develop and ask a few questions: What are the positives associated with responding in anger? When will anger cause someone to feel relieved or feel a little more in control? What are the negatives? Anger might also cause a person to feel embarrassed by having your attitude or hostility exposed in a negative light. Is this anger something that happens all the time? The anger might be something that someone experienced a while ago and continues to occur. What could have caused the anger to develop? Was it something that was trivial and unnecessary? Answering those questions can help you deal with your anger reasonably.

Short vs. Long-Term Effects

Another way to review the anger is to look at the long-term and short effects of being angry. The long-term effects could be just as harmful. Being outwardly angry might cause other people to judge you in a negative light. If they had nothing to do with the situation at the time, the anger may also cause other people to also feel angry. Examining the problems that have occurred should help understand that there are some positives involved with being angry, but those are not going to do much to help someone down the line. The situation that caused someone to become angry might be hard to understand.

Let's use an example of Ken and how he might become angry. Because of some accounting task not working as well as planned, a negative situation occurred. Ken might have thought that he was doing things right, but it turns out that he was wasting his time on the whole thing. He thought too much about certain processes and ended up failing to make the project work out. As a result, his boss became angry with him. If he wanted to, Ken could also be angry and would probably complain to his boss about it. At this point, it might be easier for him to feel frustrated due to how he spent all that time trying to manage the work that he wanted to complete. The best thing for Ken to do at this point is to get away from the situation for a few minutes. He can step out of the office for about five to ten minutes to clear his mind. Maybe he could get a bit of fresh air outdoors. After spending a bit of time collecting his thoughts, Ken can talk to his boss about the situation. He will feel more at ease as he will have a little more control over what he is thinking. He could start talking to his boss about what he did wrong and what he thought at the start. After that, the two can devise a plan to alleviate the situation and fix the problem. By getting away from the situation, Ken was able to tackle the issue again. He got over the anger and realized that he can fix the problem.

Consider the Alternatives

Being reasonable and rational is an essential part of CBT that no one should ignore. This is surely the case with managing anger. The alternative solutions to a problem can be explored in detail to see if something good can be done to keep a problem from becoming worse. In Ken's case, he would have looked at the alternatives of what he had been doing after he got mad. As he worked to calm himself down, he thought about the things that he could have done instead of becoming angry. In this case, Ken decided that he would have to talk to his boss about the situation to determine what went wrong so the issue can be resolved.

Practice Happiness or Positive Thinking

A person who becomes angry must be willing to practice happiness or think a little differently about what one wants to attain out of life and have more control over situations that could occur. A few points can be used in this process. Observe the angry feelings that you have. Identify the source of the anger. Look at what the problem is and find a positive way to spin the issue.

In Ken's example, he might notice from his work that he can learn from the errors that he made. He can concentrate on ways to correct the problem and keep it from coming up again. By turning the problem into a learning experience, he will feel happy knowing that he is doing something for himself without being hard on anyone else. It is important to release the original negative thought that occurred. Remove that old thought and replace it with the new positive spin on things. Anger can be a serious issue, and it is vital for people who are angry to see what they can do to manage the situations that they encounter. Knowing what can be done to keep anger from being a serious threat or dangerous concern to your emotions helps to improve your life while also helping someone to see that there are many ways how the anger could be corrected or controlled.

Considering the anger in question and acknowledging its presence can go a long way toward helping a person manage the issues that caused the anger.

Chapter 9 - Managing Grief through CBT

Grief is one of the most difficult emotions that any person could ever experience, and it is an emotion that all people will have to face at some point in their lives. No one can ever live forever, which makes it all the more essential to understand how to control your grief and how to stay positive even when a person reaches your darkest hour in life. When a person is in a deep state of depression, grief is a feeling that can develop. This is different from depression in that grief is typically caused not by life in general but rather by a very specific event. Grief is triggered by the death of a loved one. Whether it is the loss of a parent, a sibling, a close friend, or even a family pet, grief is painful.

The Five Stages of Grief

Grief is an emotion where a person is in deep despair and depression as a result of a painful experience. The feelings that someone develops as a result of your grief are often pervasive. To fully understand grief, it helps to understand how it progresses. There are five stages of grief, let's look at them.

Denial

In the beginning parts of grief, a person is not going to want to believe that someone has died or something irreversible has happened. This might all seem like a terrible dream, but in reality, it is indeed happening.

Anger

Sometimes, that anger is directed at people who could not do anything to resolve a problem. It may also come from your inability to correct the situation.

Bargaining

The bargaining will be unsuccessful as that person goes through more emotional pain and stress than what one might be capable of bearing.

Depression

A person will experience deep depression after realizing that the grief is real and that nothing can be done to rectify it. This is the stage where the difficult and intense sorrow has to be endured.

Acceptance

Eventually, a person will begin to accept that the grief is indeed real. It will be time to get over the situation and to finally be at peace with what has happened. This is the ultimate goal of the grief cycle. In some cases, it might be difficult for a person to finally reach the stage of acceptance. The amount of time it takes for a person to manage the situation can vary.

The Types of Grief

People experience grief in different ways. One way to understand this is by looking at the three basic types of grief that a person might experience.

Acute Grief

Acute grief occurs right after a loss and will go on for weeks or even months. People may have feelings of distress, shock, depression, and even an inability to sleep. The effects of acute grief will disappear after a while. When the acute grief is not lessening, complicated Grief occurs.

Complicated Grief

It may take years for the grief to subside. As the grief remains, it becomes harder for a person to feel happy. If they cannot move on from the grief, a person might start to feel guilty.

Integrated Grief

Integrated grief will last throughout your life and is not going to disappear. Integrated grief shows that a person still misses someone and will always grieve, but at the same time, that person will have accepted the loss and understood that it will eventually be time to move on. The problem with integrated grief is that it will often produce reminders of your loss at varying times throughout life. When someone visits a place where their loved one died or some other place that holds significance for personal reasons, this might happen. The grief may also appear during holidays and anniversaries relating to your life. The concern surrounding these forms of grief is that there is never a way for someone to truly get over the loss of a loved one. A person might appear to have got past the grief, there will always be repressed thoughts or memories attached to that person.

Common Symptoms That Accompany Grief

The symptoms that accompany your feelings of grief can be often hard and frustrating to live with. Feelings of separation may develop after having lost someone. Because a person is not capable of managing your emotions or might not be in the strongest of states, crying and sorrow can happen at random. Hallucinations might develop in some people who struggle with grief. Such hallucinations focus on things relating to the person that a person has lost. Sleeping issues may also develop. Because that someone is too busy thinking about all that has been lost, a person might not be able to get to sleep.

Using CBT to Handle Grief

There are many ways to deal with grief. When you use CBT to handle grief, there are some specific steps used. Start by addressing the thoughts of a person about grief. The thoughts that someone has surrounding grief may present as anger or denial at the beginning. The key is to help a person address the anger or other hostile feelings that one might have started having. Look at what caused the anger to develop. The odds are that anger is something that came about not from your hostility but rather from the depression. It is through your feelings of helplessness that the anger develops. Review the perception as a result of the grief. Every person perceives grief in different ways. Some people might see grief as something that is a part of life, but others might feel that it is embarrassing or unnatural. The key is to replace the attitude one has and look at examples of how people grieve. By using this alongside the rationalization one has of your grief, it becomes easier for a person to stop feeling excessively worried about grieving. Think about the attitudes that one might have that's surrounding the grief. The attitudes that are produced as a result of your grief should be inspected. This includes a review of the problems that have happened. A person should look at the situation and note the emotions one is feeling. Find relationships between each of these things to understand what might be happening in your life.

Be Grounded In the Present

The attitudes in your mind should be organized based on how grounded they might be. The goal is to look at how the mind is handling the loss and what someone might have to consider following the event. A good way to work with CBT is to think about present thoughts and plan for goals of what one can do. Your present mood may be analyzed and then adjusted over time to stay happy and in control of your emotional state. Avoid trying to keep emotions inside. This is a part of therapy that cannot be more important. Anyone who keeps their emotions inside without being able to express them could be at risk of harm as the mind struggles to maintain a sense of control and peace. These basic steps may work alongside various additional exercises such as the ones that are listed in this chapter. These include points that help someone to keep your thoughts organized and to develop a sense of recognition of whatever someone is thinking during a period of grief.

Preparing a Goodbye Worksheet

Saying goodbye to someone you love is often very difficult, but it is through this that pain that a person can move forward in the cognitive psychology process. A goodbye worksheet may be used as a guide to analyzing the feelings that someone has developed after losing a loved one. A goodbye worksheet is a CBT exercise that focuses on how well a person can respond to a situation. A worksheet should include several things. It should help you to say goodbye, and describe the feelings you have inside. This is where the emotions of grief can be revealed and the person will become familiar with the worries they are harboring. Describe some good memories of the person who has died. This may help add some peace or comfort in your mind as the past is recalled and a person feels a little better by remembering happy situations.

Document something that your loved one would certainly have wished for you to have or be. This permits even more of your feelings to come to the forefront. These worksheets are usually very challenging to do because grief is a really hard thing to deal with.

Agree to Forgive

Worksheets often include a section on forgiveness. There may have been times when a person died and left unresolved feelings due to something they have done to you. You might feel grief and anger at the same time. The objective of worksheets is to increase the state of mind by wanting to forgive. Talk with others that have been mistreated in the past. These consist of others that had people close to them pass away. This consists of the sensations that are kept in the past as an outcome of your perspectives. Be open regarding just what is taking place. Describe that there is absolutely nothing wrong with talking to others. Hear the various circumstances of others and try to empathize.

Agree to Forgive Yourself Too

A person that battles with sorrow need to forgive themselves, just as they need to forgive others. There could have been some unsolved concerns with the individual that passed away. Possibly, that individual did not have the chance to ask for forgiveness before their loved one died. You ought to be forgiven by recognizing that what may have happened in the past can't be changed and you try to be a better person and start moving on with your life. Doing this can help alliterative parts of your stress and grief.

Welcome Changes

Much of CBT has actually had to do with changing adverse concepts with favorable ones. This could certainly be stated regarding pain as it assists to change the pain gradually with something brand-new in your life. It is a smart idea to welcome something brand-new into your life to develop a feeling of positivity and happiness. There are several points that could be done to change the sensations of grief:

- Participate in some new pastimes or tasks. Such new things may be much more fun than you thought it would be.

- Traveling to someplace that creates good memories or perhaps someplace that has actually never ever been to in the past. See just what makes it a great location for somebody to go to and also take pleasure in leisure.

- Bring a new plant into your house. Having something to care for as well as to recognize somebody with is constantly a wise suggestion.

- Also getting a new family pet to take care of is a great option. An animal will certainly offer unconditional love as well as constant companionship. This could help you on a daily basis to feel better and be more effective. It is with positivity that it comes to be simpler for an individual to prevent the troubles that have pain and also to get closer to being happy and healthy in your life.

Stress Favorable Memories

The last point to do for helping with grief is to recall at the favorable memories that somebody had with an individual that was shed. This may be challenging at times since it frequently includes some of the points that one could never ever be able to experience once more. There are some points one could do. First, address any type of adverse ideas bordering your despair. Locate a favorable memory that connects to the adverse idea. This might be a trip or various other experiences that an individual had with the other individuals. Assess the memory with treatment. Take a look at some great memories. Let those positive memories stay on your mind to help soothe the harsh edge of grief. Executing this technique on a regular basis assists an individual to constantly strive to stay in a positive state of mind so that you can find joy even in grief.

A Necessary Note

As important as CBT is when dealing with pain, it is necessary to prevent trying to speed the process up. A person can form their own strategies to fight their own psychological battles. Having the ability to go on and also take care of the grief concerned is not something that any person could do instantly. It could take some time for an individual to do this. When managing somebody that is struck with despair, permit that individual to have a long time to consider the circumstance. Whatever the situation might be, it is very important to be as helpful to anyone that could have a tough time with handling their pain. Making use of CBT is important for handling your life and also maintaining despair from being a significant issue, yet it must all be done sensibly as well as with regard for the individual that requires the assistance.

Addressing Maladaptive Coping Mechanisms

Putting a stop to maladaptive coping methods is another imperative conduct measurement of CBT. As we've examined, CBT wants you to do the things that make you happy and that enhances a positive state of mind. Thus, it discourages doing things that put you in a negative headspace. Sometimes, an individual experiences anxiety, depression, or different sorts of psychological hurdles. Having positive methods for coping can help you manage your emotions and unhealthy inclinations.

For instance, taking an energetic walk when you feel on edge could be a decent coping system. Keeping away from circumstances that cause uneasiness, for example, drinking vigorously when you feel on edge is very harmful and could prompt some pretty negative consequences. Maladaptive coping components include many of the things that people do to help themselves deal with the pain like drinking intensely with the need for dulling adverse thoughts and feelings. You might use unlawful medications as well. Abusing medicine or over-the-counter prescriptions can leave you very sick and deter the whole path of your life. Using different behaviors such as sex or too much partying to change your state of mind are very common. Mentally separating from troublesome circumstances is another trap that could be fallen into. One example of avoidance is sleeping unnecessarily to try to make days end faster. A more extreme method of avoidance is engaging in self-harm.

Another example is the development of an eating disorder. Many times, people have eating disorders to give themselves some form of control when they feel that his or her life is out of order. It's important to consider what benefit your behaviors are giving you. Do they help you somehow or enable you to get away from something? Maladaptive behaviors like this are normal, and having them doesn't mean you're an awful or frail individual. Recognizing these behaviors and why you do them encourages you in two different ways. It helps you recognize when you will fall into these behaviors, and it can help you stop them at the moment they happen.

Set goals for what you hope to achieve with CBT. Goals should be specific, measurable, and achievable. In other words, focus on the changes that would be really meaningful to you to achieve within the next few weeks or months, and think about how you will know when you have achieved those changes. For example, avoid setting goals like "Feel less depressed" or "Stop feeling worried." Instead, state what you want to feel more of "Feel more energetic, hopeful, and so on" as well as what that would look like to you, such as "Get up early three to four mornings each week feeling happier" and "Do leisure activities that I enjoy three days each week." Goals could also relate to facing situations that cause anxiety- like "Beginning in two weeks, speak up in class/ meetings three to four times per week" or intrusive thoughts like "Reduce the distress associated with intrusive thoughts by half."

Avoid setting goals that require big, immediate changes or doing something every single day. If you are trying to begin exercising to improve mood and overall health, start by aiming for a thirty-minute walk four times per week, rather than running for one hour every day. Unreasonable goals can create a sense of failure when you don't achieve them right away. If you wish, you can set goals for the short, medium, and long-term that reflects both reasonable expectations for the present and high hopes for the future. You can set long-term goals as far out as a few years into the future, but make sure you have achievable goals in the next few weeks as well. It may be helpful to identify broad areas such as family, health, and work, and then identify specific goals within those areas.

You may also wish to prioritize your goals and start by focusing on those you feel are most important or most achievable. Make sure any goal you set is truly meaningful to you. If you realize that one of your goals doesn't feel important, try refining it or discarding it all together. Whether you're struggling with negative self-image, social anxiety and/or an avoidance of group activities you used to enjoy, two goals might be 1) to develop a more balanced view of yourself and trust in your ability to positively interact with others, and 2) to start attending social events again or to commit yourself to a regular social activity. Once you have outlined your goals, it is important to describe what steps are needed to reach them in concrete terms. For someone with social anxiety, for example, the steps might look something like this: Learn two strategies to challenge negative self-talk.

Chapter 10 - CBT Can Help You Strive For Happiness

Happiness always exists within us. You might think to yourself "I am often aware that I am unhappy but do not always feel that I am searching". The absence of peace and happiness is the experience we know as suffering or unhappiness and is always accompanied by a search to recover them. It is not possible to be suffering and not to be in search of peace and happiness. In reality, we do not actually lack anything, our happiness is still there, but it is buried under our pain.

One of the most common reasons people give for their unhappiness is that the world is so truly awful, so full of suffering and pain, that one would have to be a blind fool to be happy in a world such as this. This may seem a pretty convincing argument and to a certain degree it is true, the world is imperfect and people often do awful things to each other. You never have to look very far to find someone being dishonest, selfish, angry, greedy, or cruel. Some people feel that to be happy in the face of such human failings would be living in denial or mean that they lacked compassion or empathy, or are somehow ignorant of the plight of those who suffer at the hands others. But if one looks closely at what is the root cause of people's bad behavior it becomes so clear. People only behave badly when they are not happy. No one steals unless they want something they do not have. No one lies unless they are unhappy with the truth. Happy people do not erupt into violence. Happy people do not kill, rape, abuse or disregard others. All human folly arises as a result of people not being happy, either because they want something they do not have, they don't want something they do have, or they want to feel a way they do not feel. It is no small irony that many people feel they cannot be happy when there are so many people in the world behaving with such appallingly disregard for others. But when you get right down to it, it is a profound lack of happiness that is the root cause of all antisocial behavior. If you search your memory for all the times when you have acted in a less than noble fashion, you will pretty soon realize it's true. All of your lowest acts were born out of a deep sense of desire or dissatisfaction. No one ever harms others unless they are covetous, unsettled, or miserable within themselves. Conversely, happy people are loving, kind, generous, helpful, and compassionate; all the things the world needs more of. Happy people consider others. Happy people go out of their way to help others. Happy people feel full and content and have plenty left over for others. All the best things people do are the product of happiness, goodwill and a generosity of spirit.

People give many reasons for not being happy but mostly we attribute our misery to something that has occurred outside of ourselves. Anything that happens out in the big wide world that we do not like and we immediately jump into the victim's mentality. On the face of it, these arguments appear to have some merit, but is it really true? Unwanted things happen to everyone. Do you know of anyone who leads a life totally devoid of disappointment or conflict? It's just not possible to control the world so that we always get what we want or so that nobody ever insults, abuses, refuses, or denies us. It is important to choose happiness anyway.

Chapter 11 - The Art of Journaling

Individuals like to be imaginative. They enjoy lots of one-of-a-kind points they wish to create. Whether it is writing songs or books, there are several methods individuals could generate imaginative points and also share their concepts in a manner in which they may have never ever thought of in the past. One such method individuals could do this is by journaling. Journaling is an extremely obvious method that any person could utilize. It is a technique where an individual will certainly create numerous points in a publication with every one of the factors connecting to exactly what a person has actually done on a normal day. This is a method that has actually been utilized by individuals of all kinds as well as all ages due to the fact of how very easy it could be to generate a distinctive tale. Journaling might function well for individuals that are attempting to manage their anxieties, sensations of clinical depression, or the sorrow that they could really feel. The actions of the journal are necessary to evaluate. When a person is experiencing some kind of terrible situation, it makes it harder for the body to react and also really feel comfortable.

Let's take a look at the story of Tony. He's a high school student. He always had a hard time with public speaking that he had actually battled to finish public speeches. He is always nervous the days leading up to a speech. Tony wants to get rid of the anxiousness that happens when he is working on his speech and the anger that happens when it all falls apart. He starts writing a journal to make it easier to figure out the source of his fear. Tony would certainly write about just how he had a challenging time aiming to finish a speech in the class. He would certainly clarify in as much information as feasible just how challenging the speech was as well as exactly what he attempted to do to preserve your honor.

The very first ideas that Tony had needs several things to be done. He has to discuss these sensations despite exactly how extreme or deep they could have been. The origin of his reasoning must be checked out. He has to think of previous occasions prior to that which resulted in him experiencing that emotion towards public speaking. By examining the effects of the occasion, Tony will certainly observe what changes he should make. If he does not keep his mind under control, he understands that his speech quality and also his social standing can both be damaged. Tony will certainly figure out why he feels his actions were necessary. As he takes a look at just how he was dismayed with his speech, he will certainly begin to discover that those sensations will just make him come to be much more irritated or distressed.

Next, Tony thinks about new methods to perfect his speeches. If he concentrated much more on the speech as a whole instead compared to battling with simply one facet, he would certainly recognize that his classmates could be much more responsive. If he concentrates on just what he desires to do, Tony will create an affirmation that he is qualified for doing anything. The following activities that Tony thought of simply a minute ago needs to be made use on the next speech he will make. He could consider the whole speech as well as concentrate on being great rather than simply concentrating on bad thing that will most probably not happen. When looking at how individuals react to his speech, he would be much less hard of himself.

What Sorts of Subjects Can Be Covered In a Journal?

The very best component of journaling for CBT is that the method could be regarding any type of subject. Making the journal rewarding should be practical or sensible. An individual may have a wish to write about methods of exactly how a person could settle particular economic concerns. An individual may want to go back to school and learn more about the economy. This is a sensible strategy. An individual could additionally write about winning the lotto or having an inheritance from a relative. Those are intriguing elements of handling economic troubles. However, they are not reasonable. The total objective is to infuse a feeling of hope in your life. Locating methods to make the mind really feel better as well as more powerful is the main objective.

Write details in a journal about your fears and anxiety. You should include details on what happened when uncertainty was felt and what was done to respond to the concerns at the time. Your feelings can also be noted. Was the situation easier to get through than what one thought or was it a challenge? Discuss the things that happened and be as specific as possible. List the results of all those events that took place. Talk about what happened and if things went well or did not. Review anything that happened in the event that a situation did not turn out the way it was planned. When something wrong happened, explain what happened. Being able to contextualize the anxiety in a journal will help to understand how well one is using CBT to manage anxiety. Identify how well one coped with uncertainty. The person should discuss how well things turned out, particularly if the situation came out just fine and nothing untoward happened. Sometimes, the situation at hand will not be significant.

In other cases, a person might have got into some trouble and is trying to cope with the outcome. Being able to handle the outcome can be a challenge to manage. The results of the situation should determine how well a person is able to cope with a situation and if that someone is capable of managing anxiety in even the most negative situations or events that might happen in the future. Anxiety does not have to affect every part of your life. Working with an open plan and an organized routine is vital to understand that nothing can ever be truly predicted. Being realistic can make an impact on how well someone feels about a situation.

When you are writing in your journal, you could fall into the trap of thinking that thoughts or actions are simply either "good" or "bad." It is best to use more descriptive words that might be more generous or honest in nature. Saying that a thought was "helpful" or "unhelpful" might be a better choice.

Get Back to the Present

After looking at the situation, return to the present and think about what is going on right now. Avoid looking back into the past and replace the thoughts with something more efficient or productive. The issues that someone has should be defused at this point. The difficult problems one has can be kept from being otherwise likely or pervasive to grow or thrive. The best part of the process is that it only takes a few seconds for this to work.

Practicing Positive Thoughts

Tony wants to enhance his skills of making speeches and confidently saying it out loud in the public. The next thing Tony should do is to consider brand new methods to practice his speech. His newly discovered method should be used in his new speeches. He could describe that he really felt much better, as well as extra positive concerning the speech that he made. By utilizing his journal, Tony will certainly observe the psychological procedures he is utilizing as well as just how they are determining exactly what he does with his speeches.

If you're enjoying this book, I would appreciate it if you went to the place of purchase and left a short positive review. Thank you.

Chapter 12 - Should a Psychiatrist Be Consulted?

Everything listed in this guide on Cognitive Behavioral Therapy is easy and simple to follow on your own. This could help people to manage their lives and emotions without having to consult a psychiatrist for help. That does not mean that a psychiatrist is always unnecessary. People who need emotional help might still require a psychiatrist for extra guidance in the cognitive psychology process. Because they are so concerned about their image, many people are afraid to ask for this help. However, there are times when a psychiatrist needs to be consulted.

The greatest problem is that the effort might be pervasive and too intense. That is, a person keeps on having to use the same strategies for using their mind all day long without stopping. This is a frustrating feeling, and it is a problem that will remain hard and troubling for many to live with. When that effort does not work and does not produce results, it might be time to get in touch with a psychiatrist for added help.

Obsessions Become Too Prominent

CBT is to be used to help get people over their obsessive thoughts and allow new positive thoughts to come into play in your life. There are, oftentimes, when the obsessions could become too intense. The old worries that someone had might be so strong and a person will start to think too often about certain problems or worries in life. The obsessions might include obsessions to be perfect or having the same thoughts repeatedly running on a person's head even after an activity was done. Such a problem might be a sign of something a little more intense in your mind and would, therefore, require a professional to provide more help in dealing with the obsession so that it does not take over a person's life.

Consulting a Therapist

Sometimes, a person might continue to have thoughts of consulting a therapist even while using many of the strategies in this book. These thoughts might be a sign that someone is fearful of a process not working. It might suggest that a process is not as strong as one might have wished it could be. Repetitive thoughts of consulting a therapist for help might be an indication that a therapist should be consulted. People talk about their need for a psychiatrist even when someone tries to do things and change your thinking. They might still have many visible problems that others may notice. The greatest problem here is that the person who needs help might not be fully aware of the problems that they have. Other people might notice the concerns that a person has, but the person who suffers the condition does not. Anyone who hears requests about getting help should probably ask for that help.

Feelings Aren't Getting Better

Contacting a therapist is often a necessity for cases where the negative feelings one has are not changing. The points listed here should help people to change their lives and to make them feel stronger and more confident. When the traditional processes one uses are not working, it is best to consult a therapist for help. This is especially for cases where feelings of depression or other serious emotional problems continue to get worse and harder to manage. When talking with a psychiatrist, a person will not likely be required with medications. Many of today's psychiatrists are willing to help people find strategies for living that work without the need for any medications. Medication might still be prescribed for cases where a physical imbalance might appear in your brain or a person's mental concerns are serious enough which makes someone be at a risk of self-harm. All psychiatrists focus on ensuring their patients are safe.

People who work to improve their lives are always trying to change their thoughts. By doing this, it becomes easier for the mind to evolve and grow. It is through your emotional problems that one learns what can be done to get the problems one has managed. Cognitive psychology is a practice that helps people to understand how to thrive in life and make the work one puts in worthwhile. With CBT, a person will have more control over your thoughts. Because someone knows how to manage the positive ones and to keep the negative issues in your mind from being a dramatic threat, the thoughts will be easy to manage. The fears that one might experience can be alleviated through CBT. The practice allows anyone to think twice about the fears one has and how they can hinder your way of living a comfortable life. This includes an emphasis on knowing how fears are formed and how to gradually correct them before they can become a burden.

CBT also works to relieve anxiety and for a person to recognize how irrational some anxiety-related triggers are. Many fears are not as strong as one might think and the anxieties produced by them are not things to be concerned about. Some of the saddest feelings can be managed through CBT. When the right ideas for regulating the mind and your thoughts are introduced, depression does not have to be a burden. Grief can be kept in check by using some constructive points and smart ideas to move on with life and to keep grief from crippling your way of living.

People Talk About Your Need for a Psychiatrist

Even when someone tries to do things and change their thinking, they might still have many visible problems that others may notice. It is through your emotional problems that one learns what can be done to get the problems one has managed. The thoughts will be easy to manage because they know how to thinks positive ones and to keep the negative issues in your mind from being a dramatic threat. The practice allows anyone to think twice about the fears one has and how they can hinder your way of living a comfortable life. Every instance of how CBT may work varies by person, so knowing what to expect out of the process will be essential to your success in keeping your life in check.

Chapter 13 - Living a Healthy Lifestyle

Sleep

There are things you will do in your life outside the CBT methods that may greatly help your well-being and increase the effectiveness of any therapy you utilize. One vital factor is sleep. Having enough sleep is important for mood, energy levels, physical ¬health, and even the health of the brain. Things like anxiety will make it difficult to sleep, making a reinforcing cycle of stress and exhaustion. However, there are several straightforward changes you'll create to help yourself get a decent night's sleep, such as attempt to sleep and wake up at a similar time every day and to sleep after you feel tired. Don't oversleep to make up for lost sleep. Don't watch TV, use your phone, or dine in bed. Offer yourself thirty minutes to an hour before bed to relax. Get physical activity throughout the day, it could help you sleep better at night.

Healthy Eating

Many of us realize that a healthier diet contributes to a more robust sense of overall well-being. It can even contribute to weight loss and improvement of different health factors, relieving anxiety within the method. If you're feeling that addressing your diet currently would result in a lot of anxiety, leave it for a later time. However, if you're feeling driven to enhance your diet, go for it. It may be the thing you need to feel healthier and less anxious or depressed. You should merely aim to eat a lot of fruit, vegetables, whole grains, fish, healthy fats like oil and avocado, nuts, and seeds, and less white meat, high-fat dairy farm, white flour and refined grains, sugars, change oils, and processed foods generally. If you love cooking, taking cooking lessons and creating healthier home-cooked meals may well be a good a part of your behavioral-activation strategy.

Physical Activity

Physical activity is the simplest way to enhance mood. Physical activity doesn't have to mean exercise. Many of us believe that they need to move to the gym and run on a treadmill or ride a stationary bike for it to count. This is mostly not true! There are several other ways to be active that doesn't involve going to the gym. Walking, biking, and hiking outside is fun and restful, and many believe that walking and standing more can help you live a longer life.

Low-intensity activities like gardening, playing catch together with your kid, doing yard work, or actively cleaning the house up are great options.

Meditation

Meditation could be a good way to alleviate stress and cultivate attentiveness. There are several approaches that can be used. One simple option is to begin a mantra meditation. It's a type of meditation during which one chooses a sound or phrase and repeats it for a number of times. It is as straightforward as a soothing sound, like "om" or "ahh," or it is a phrase in any language expressing sentiments of compassion, kindness, or peace. You'll need to make one up yourself or use a conventional ancient mantra that has been murmured for hundreds of years. There's extremely nice flexibility in mantra meditation. Make sure to choose a mantra that is soothing and can assist you in clearing your mind throughout meditation. If you are interested in mantras and meditation, there are several videos online that may assist you in providing you with the proper methods and meditation examples.

If you want, you could shift to silent meditation. For those that follow a religion, repetitive contemplation of any prayer or passage from scripture is very effective. Select any passage from your holy book. You can read or chant it repeatedly. While you do that, make sure to relish every word and each phrase. Take the time to hear yourself as you recite the passage. What insights and reflections will it awaken in you? Watch your response to your prayer, and after you are done, pay attention to yourself in complete silence. To get the most out of your mediation, try to it on a daily basis. Attempt to put aside ten to fifteen minutes every day to try other kinds of mantra meditation. If you can't, that's okay. Just do the best that you can.

Nature Therapy

Recent studies have found that interacting with nature on a daily basis has a tremendous impact on our sense of health, happiness, and well-being. You don't have to do any intense running or hiking, you could just sit in a pretty clearing, or sketching a beautiful scene in the nature around you. Getting sun and fresh air has a major effect on stress levels. If you reside close to a forest, like a state park, put aside an hour or so for a visit. If not, you'll get similar benefits from a town park with trees and a green grass. It doesn't specifically have to be a forest either. A meadow, a big backyard, a river, or any outside space you discover stunning and soothing can do. Create a way to immerse yourself within the outdoor space. Close up your phone or leave it in your car. Interact all of your senses within the experience. Take notice of the smell of the soil, the air, and plants, the sounds of wind, water, and animals, the feel of leaves and bark, and also the feel of the earth below your feet. Relish the brilliant colors and look at all the flowers, maybe even jots down the color and look of any you find particularly beautiful.

Bird-Watching

Bird-watching could be a tremendous way to get away. You can feel completely immersed within the experience of being outside since you're going to be really focused on every flash of color and each rustle or sound. It's precisely this type of complete interaction with nature that helps relieve stress and boost your everyday mood. It additionally helps you to marvel at nature, as you develop an appreciation for the various kinds of birds and their distinctive habits. If you're already a bird watcher, create a degree to travel out a least a number of times per month. Visit new locations, and listen to seasonal migrations that will offer you an opportunity to examine new birds. Bird watching is additionally a good activity to do on vacations since several stunning natural areas around the world boast numerous bird and wildlife as well as cater to bird watchers. Even if you haven't ever gone bird watching before, it's a straightforward hobby that is easy to get started with. All you'll have to need is some binoculars and either your phone or a book to help you identify the birds you see. Then head to a park, or maybe an oversized yard, and see what kinds of birds you'll see. Wherever you reside, you could possibly attract several kinds of birds with feeders you can hang near your home.

Disorders like anxiety and depression tend to be rampant in America. As people, we tend to become excessively focus on ourselves. This typically comes from being overwhelmed—the emotions that we tend to feel are unable to influence our current reality. This could lead to emotional dysfunction within the face of things that aren't really threatening. Our individual worlds become nerve-racking and demand a lot of our attention. However, it doesn't mean that we are not generous or we tend to not care about other people. You are by no means a "bad person" for feeling like this! Being overwhelmed could be a common symptom of the many mental diseases and disorders. This intense self-focus could be a type of suffering caused by anxiety or depression and not merely an indication of selfishness. In fact, we tend to typically care deeply for the people we love and feel badly that we tend to not be as responsive or caring as we might wish to be. It becomes analytic, and isolation is excruciating for humans. Humans are naturally social creatures. We tend to relish the sense of happiness. We tend to be the most satisfied and we care deeply about the connections with others and their well-being.

Gaining perspective

There are great ways to gain perspective and feel better that complement CBT. Let's look at some examples of things that you can incorporate in your daily life to keep a positive perspective.

Nature
We've already talked regarding a number of the advantages of being in nature for stress reduction. Experiencing stunning sunsets, mountains, waterfalls, rolling waves, beautiful coastlines, big

trees, and wondrous animal life will cause you to feel connected to the rest of the living world. Think about the fact that the mountains you're standing on are there for thousands of years, that the tree lofty higher than you is formed from small cells distantly involving your own, or that the birds stopping to rest in your yard migrate thousands of miles will offer perspective and shift your focus from aspects of your life that you simply understand as negative. If you've got vacation time, create a plan to travel somewhere with natural beauty, whether or not it's on the opposite side of the globe or simply an hour away at a nature reserve. If you prefer exciting activities, do something exhilarating during a trip like mountain biking, paragliding, or windsurfing. Walking, hiking, cycling, horseback riding, or just resting within the presence of beautiful natural options will fill you with a sense of awe and place things in perspective. Looking at a visually beautiful documentary can even inspire a way of awe regarding nature.

Art and Music

The sweetness and depth of human expression through art and music is moving and awe-inspiring. Listen to singers whose voices you discover really distinctive and exquisite. Go to an opera or a symphony with an awesome, sweeping finale. Explore paintings and sculptures that are beautiful in their ability to capture feelings. Read poetry that touches you with its sincerity and creativeness. If no artists or artworks come to mind immediately, that's okay. Consider art and music as a therapeutic path to explore, with the goal of discovering a number of creations that inspire you.

Chapter 14 - Problem Solving

Problem-solving is great when a circumstance can be changed, but that change might be laden with tension. Problems may likewise be associated with sadness, medical issues, drug and alcohol dependence, or family issues. Some sorts of problems that could be having no proper communication your life partner, paying off your bills, starting a new diet, or striving to stop smoking.

This methodology isn't proper for all problems. In the event that you are experiencing extreme sadness or genuine psychological instability, this methodology won't be sufficient for these issues. Now and again, there isn't an answer to every problem. Problem-solving will sometimes just give you ways of dealing with stress so that you will be able to live with it. This is called emotion-focused coping and it can help give you a more solid feeling of control and confidence. There are is a plan within CBT to help you with problem-solving. Let's look at CBT's approach.

The problem-solving approach educated with CBT has seven steps:

Step 1: Identify the Problem

The first step is to understand the problem in detail. Write down your problem and how you think your plan will fix that problem. Stick to the facts of the problem, so that your plan can be both actionable and reasonable.

Step 2: Identify Reasonable Plans

Think about your goals. Try not to worry about them being perfect. Just stay reasonable in your plans. If you do make some plans that later doesn't seem feasible, you can always change them down the road.

Step 3: Evaluate Your Plans

When you have a couple of realistic plans, record the advantages and disadvantages of each one. You can reach out to friends and family for help and feedback.

Step 4: Decide on Ideal and Backup Plans

In view of the advantages and disadvantages of the conceivable plans, settle on the best plan and a couple of backup plans.

Step 5: Plan What You Have to Do

Plan out the small steps involved in your plan. Separating it into little steps can make it more manageable.

Step 6: Carry Out Your Plan

Do the steps you recorded in Step 5. If necessary, move to one of your backup plans.

Step 7: Review and Change Plan as Required

How could it go? Is the problem solved decreased to a more reasonable level? If the problem isn't solved or if another problem has emerged, you can come back to Step 1 and figure another plan. You can do this as often as you need to.

The many things that have been covered in this guide deserve to be noticed. There are a few final tips that need to be discussed when aiming to get the most out of the cognitive behavioral therapy process.

Always Have a Goal

A clear-cut goal will include a clear objective. The goal can be anything that someone one wants to do so long as it is positive and reasonable. The goal can be a long-term or short one. The goal must be clearly defined and realistic regardless of the type of situation that one encounters.

Every Situation Is Unique

Overgeneralization and other distortions are often things that people will encounter. These problems often make it harder for people to plan smart ideas or thoughts. People need to recognize that the situations are always different. People might look at the circumstances including a review of each situation based on the setting, the people who are involved, and any other things that might trigger changes. People should avoid personalizing the situations. Personalizing can disrupt your train of thought. Don't assume everything is about oneself.

Determine the Proper Definitions

Every attitude or emotion that one has will come with a distinct definition. When figuring out how well CBT can work, it is up to a person to recognize the certain definitions that one wishes to follow. A person might have your own idea for what disappointment is like. There could be a difference between the objectives that one has and the expectations involved. Understanding what disappointment is really like in your mind can be essential for handling your values and ideas. When resolving emotional problems, there is a need to think carefully about the definitions that will be used to ensure there are no problems with what one will be doing.

Never Blame Others

The goal of cognitive psychology is to help people recognize what they are doing for themselves and how they can be better people without being hard on others. Much of this involves ensuring that other people are not blamed for the things that one might do or say. It is very easy to pass off the responsibility of a situation to someone else. Blaming is a frequent practice that is easy to do, but it only shows a lack of responsibility. It suggests that instead of being willing to accept a situation for what it is, someone will instead think more about the problems that have developed. The best thing to do in this situation is to be accepting of whatever has come your way. It is not productive to blame others for everything that happens.

Never Be Overly Judgmental

It is understandable why people might be hard on themselves. They have their own worries or fears and they want to make what they are doing work well. The work that someone puts into CBT can only go so far as one wants it to go. Having a useful and smart plan on hand for therapy can make a real change in your life.

Conclusion

All of the points in this guide are suitable for many needs. They all require introspection and effort on a person's part to work. Those who are committed to the therapeutic process will find that it is not hard to get more out of the practice. Be aware of how much time and control it might take to resolve certain emotional issues. Look at the work being put into the process and see what can be done to manage life in a constructive fashion. Always be aware of the situation one enters into and how challenging the problem might be. Every instance of how CBT may work varies by person, so knowing what to expect out of the process will be essential to your success in keeping your life in check. Most importantly, be patient when using CBT. Every person responds to CBT uniquely. It might take weeks or even months to make cognitive progress. The effects of the process can last a lifetime and will allow a person to feel better about any situation one encounter. Good luck with using the points highlighted in this guide. When the best strategies and ideas for the concern are used, it is easy to keep fears, depression, and other negative aspects of your life from being overly influential.

Printed in Poland
by Amazon Fulfillment
Poland Sp. z o.o., Wrocław